INVESTIGATING HISTORY

BRITAIN, 1750–1900

John D. Clare

Hodder & Stoughton

A MEMBER OF THE HODDER HEADLINE GROUP

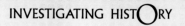
Acknowledgements

The publishers would like to thank the following individuals, institutions and companies for permission to reproduce copyright illustrations in this book:

Mary Evans: pp4, 6, 9 (l), 10 (b), 16, 22, 24, 29 (t and b), 32, 33, 47, 50, 68 (t), 69, 70, 73, 82; Punch: pp5, 66, 75, 84; Bridgeman Art Library: pp7, 10(t) (View of the Iron bridge, 1780 by William Williams (1740–1800) Ironbridge Gorge Museum, Telford, Shropshire, UK), 21 (Coalbrookdale by Night, 1808 (oil on canvas) by Philip James Loutherbourg (Jacques) de (1740–1812) Science Museum, London, UK), 39 (t) (Buckingham Palace: from St. James's Park, 1842 (litho) by Thomas Shotter Boys (1803–74) Guidhall Library, Corporation of London, UK), 40 (b) (Applicants for Admission to a Casual Ward, 1874 (oil on canvas) by Sir Samuel Luke Fildes (1844–1927) Royal Holloway), 41 (Hush! (The Concert) c. 1875 (oil on canvas) by James Jacques Tissot 91836-19020 Manchester Art Gallery, UK), 46 (Christ in the House of His Parents, 1863 (oil on canvas) by J. E. Millais (1829–96) & Solomon (1832–1886) Private Collection), 59 (The Election III The Polling, 1754–55 by William Hogarth (1697–1764) Courtesy of the Trustees of Sir John Soane's Museum, London), 65 (panel) by English School (18th century) Royal College of Surgeons, London, UK), 89; Topham Picturepoint: pp9 (r), 13, 30 (t, l), 40 (t), 49, 57, 90; CORBIS: pp11 (Jason Hawkes), 12 (© National Gallery Collection; By kind permission of the Trustees of the National Gallery, London), 14, 36 and 53 (Hulton-Deutsch Collection), 17 (t) and 55 (Historical Picture Archive), 39 (b) (Stapleton Collection), 78, 80–81 (Bojan Brecelj), 86 (Michael Masian Historic Photographs); British Museum, Department of prints and drawings: p19 (Cruikshank Tremendous Sacrifice Series); PA Photos: p23; Mansell/Timepix/Rex Features: p25; Manchester Public Libraries: pp27 (JR Barfoots: "Progress of Cotton" Plate 6 "Spinning"), p60; R.J Heald c/o Saltaire Tourist Information and Gift Centre Ltd, www.saltaire.yorks.com/touristinfo: pp30 (t; m and r) (b; l, m and l), 31 (all); Toledo Museum of Art: p35 (James Tissot (French, 1836–1902), London Visitors, 1874, oil on canvas, 63x 45 inches. (160 x 114.2cm) purchased with funds from the Libbey Endowment, Gift of Edward Drommond Libbey); AKG Photo: p38; Tate Gallery: pp43 (Henry Alexander Bowler (1824– 1903) The Doubt: Can these Dry Bones Live? 1855 (oil on canvas)), 44 (William Holam Hunt (1827–1910) The Awakening of Conscience, 1853 (oil on canvas)), 67 (Sir Luke Fildes (1843–1927) The Doctor, 1891 (oil on canvas)); Hulton Getty: pp56, 71; Centre for the Study of Cartoons and Caricature, University of Kent, Canterbury, CT2 7NU: p62 (W.K. Haselden, Daily Mirror, 15 April, 1907); The British Museum: p68 (b) (© Bank of England); BoondocksNet.com: p77; Boston Irish Tourism Association: p83; British Library: pp87(#703/16), 88 (# 430/17 (33) © India Office); The Kobal Collection/20th Century Fox: p92.

Every effort has been made to trace and acknowledge ownership of copyright. The publishers will be glad to make suitable arrangements with any copyright holders whom it has not been possible to contact.

Note about the Internet links in the book. The user should be aware that URLs or web addresses change regularly. Every effort has been made to ensure the accuracy of the URLs provided in this book on going to press. It is inevitable, however, that some will change. It is sometimes possible to find a relocated web page, by just typing in the address of the home page for a website in the URL window of your browser.

Artworks by Chris Rothero (Beehive Illustration) and Richard Morris.

Orders: please contact Bookpoint Ltd, 130 Milton Park, Abingdon, Oxon OX14 4SB. Telephone: (44) 01235 827720. Fax: (44) 01235 400454. Lines are open from 9.00 - 6.00, Monday to Saturday, with a 24 hour message answering service. You can also order through our website www.hodderheadline.co.uk.

British Library Cataloguing in Publication Data
A catalogue record for this title is available from the British Library

ISBN 0 340 86910 0

First Published 2003
Impression number   10 9 8 7 6 5 4 3 2
Year   2009 2008 2007 2006 2005 2004

Cover photo shows the painting: "Work" by Ford Maddox Brown, 1863 supplied by the Bridgeman Art Library.
Layout by Lorraine Inglis Design.
Originated by Dot Gradations Ltd, UK
Printed in Italy for Hodder & Stoughton Educational, a division of Hodder Headline, 338 Euston Road, London NW1 3BH

CONTENTS

INTRODUCTION

What can Jack the Ripper tell us?

SOURCE Ⓐ

Whitechapel, drawn by the French engraver Gustav Doré in 1870.

On 6 August 1888 Martha Tabram, a Whitechapel **prostitute**, was found murdered. She had been stabbed 39 times on 'body, neck and private parts'. On 31 August, Mary Ann Nichols was found with her throat slit; her abdomen had been mutilated with a long knife.

Then on 8 September, another prostitute, 'Dark Annie' Chapman, was found murdered – her throat had been slit, and her intestines and organs removed. The police surgeon suggested that the cuts had been made by a professional – a doctor or a butcher.

Whitechapel in 1888 was a sink of poverty and crime. Of the 76,000 inhabitants, 40% lived below the poverty line. Around 8500 people slept in one of the 233 lodging houses. Half the population were poor Jewish immigrants, but Irish, Russians, Poles and many other races lived there. There were (at least) 1200 prostitutes. The Victorians believed that soldiers needed prostitutes, and the Contagious Diseases Act gave police the right to arrest and brutally examine prostitutes to make sure they were 'clean'.

On 30 September, two more prostitutes – Elizabeth Stride and Catherine Eddowes – were murdered and mutilated within minutes of each other. A mis-spelled notice on a doorway read: 'The Juwes [Jews] are The men That Will not be Blamed For nothing'. Fearing anti-Jewish riots, the police washed it off immediately.

On 16 October a letter and a piece of human kidney were sent to the police (see Source C). Next month another prostitute, Mary Kelly, was horribly murdered.

The police were baffled.

THINK ABOUT IT

Write about the scene in Source A, describing:

- the people
- the environment
- the atmosphere.

'Painting a picture with words' will involve the use of the language of description – including well-chosen verbs and adjectives, metaphors and similes.

SOURCE B

Whitechapel

The spirit of murder hovers over this spot, for life is held of little account. Down from one dark court rings a cry of murder, and a woman, her face hideously gashed, makes across the narrow road, pursued by a howling madman. It is only a drunken husband having a row with his wife.

George Sims, How the Poor Live *(1889).*

SOURCE C

Sor

I send you half the Kidne I took from one women prasarved it for you tother piece I fried and ate it was very nise I may send you the bloody knif that took it out if you only wate a whil longer

Signed

Catch me when You can

Anonymous letter, sent to the police on 16 October 1888.

◆ *This letter was accompanied by a piece of human kidney. The police were unable to tell if the letter came from the real killer or if the kidney came from one of the murdered women.*

BLIND-MAN'S BUFF.
(As played by the Police.)
" TURN ROUND THREE TIMES,
AND CATCH WHOM YOU MAY ! "

SOURCE E

This cartoon is from Punch, *September 1888. What is it suggesting about the police?*

SOURCE D

London's Police in Victorian times were operating in a knowledge vacuum with no modern forensic tools available to them. Fingerprinting, blood typing and other staples of forensic technique were not yet developed for police use.

Marilyn Bardsley, Jack the Ripper.

THINK ABOUT IT

1. Sources D and E give different explanations why the police could not catch the Ripper. What reasons do they suggest?

2. Suggest reasons why they give the explanations they do.

The crimes created a sensation. Newspapers were full of the 'hideous murders'. Since the victims were women, Queen Victoria intervened and demanded that the killer be found.

The police distributed 80,000 handbills, and questioned 2000 people, including sailors from the docks, Asians in London's opium dens, Greek gypsies, cowboys from the American Exhibition and 76 butchers.

The mentally ill were especially suspect, and the police later named the three most likely suspects – a **syphilitic** doctor, an insane Pole, and a mad Russian doctor. Foreigners were also suspect – *The Times* thought that the crimes were 'inconsistent with the calm English nature'. Similarly, Police Chief Inspector Abberline felt that 'sexual maniacs of the type of the "Ripper" were more likely to be found in Europe, or in Asia, than in Britain'.

Most wealthier people, however, agreed with *The Lancet* which, on 6 October, blamed 'great poverty, overcrowding, dirt, and bad **sanitation**'.

The poor people of Whitechapel had other theories. They claimed that the killer was well-to-do – probably a doctor. Some even claimed that the Ripper was Queen Victoria's grandson, Prince Albert Victor, who frequented the gay brothels of Whitechapel.

After Mary Kelly, the Ripper never struck again. Nobody has ever been able to discover who committed the dreadful deeds of that fearful summer of 1888.

The story of Jack the Ripper opens for us a 'window' into the past. This book will study the forces that created a world where such a thing could happen.

A picture from a French newspaper.

THINK ABOUT IT

1. Discuss with a partner or in a group what the story of Jack the Ripper tells historians about:

   - Attitudes to the poor.
   - Living conditions in parts of London, and the gap between rich and poor.
   - Public attitudes to sex and morality.
   - Politics, the monarchy, and the pressure of public opinion.
   - Medical knowledge at that time.
   - Attitudes to the Army, and to foreigners.

2. Remember your study of Tudor and Stuart Britain. Using the six bullet points above, suggest aspects of the story of Jack the Ripper that could or would never have happened in 1688.

STOP AND REFLECT: Write notes under six bullet points to explain what the story of Jack the Ripper tells historians about Britain in the late nineteenth century.

CHAPTER 1

An Age of Wonder

How did the Victorians feel about the Industrial Revolution?

In this chapter you will:

- Find out which areas of the economy developed during the Industrial Revolution.
- Study what the Victorians thought about the developments of the Industrial Revolution.
- Write an imaginary letter showing Victorian attitudes to the Great Exhibition.

SOURCE A

This picture, Work, *painted by Ford Madox Brown in 1863, shows navvies laying water pipes. Notice:*
- *the beer-seller, his eye bruised in a fight*
- *the orphan girl, acting as mother to her brothers and sisters*
- *the medicinal herbs seller*
- *rich people at the top of the painting, poor people at the bottom.*

The two men watching on the right are Rev F D Maurice, who founded a Working Men's College, and the historian Thomas Carlyle.

THINK ABOUT IT

1. Make a list of everything that is happening in Source A. What does the picture tell us about the Victorians' attitude to life?

2. Why, do you think, does Brown have Maurice and Carlyle watching the scene?

Between 1750 and 1900 there was an **Industrial Revolution**. Almost everything you see around you in terms of technology and industry owes its origin to these years of growth and development. For most of the nineteenth century Britain was 'the workshop of the world' and – based upon her industrial strength – built an Empire which covered a fifth of the globe.

The Victorians were amazed by their achievements. They were fascinated by marvels – and the more shocking, the better. They genuinely believed they were near perfection – in 1851 Prince Albert told one audience that 'man is approaching a fulfilment of that great and sacred mission … to conquer nature to his use; himself a divine instrument'.

SOURCE B

This terrifying Victorian invention (1891) was designed for people who enjoyed 'unnerving sensations'. The idea was to drop the capsule from the top of the Eiffel Tower – it was calculated that the gigantic shell would achieve 172 miles per hour.

'It has hitherto been doubtful whether one could do this and survive,' said the inventor, but he assured his readers that they would be saved by the pool of water below the Tower, and that the springs in the shell would act as a shock-absorber.

The scheme was never tried.

SOURCE C

Progress

A young man, alive at this period, hardly knows to what improvements of human life he has been introduced. Gas was unknown: I groped about the streets of London in all but the utter darkness of a twinkling oil lamp.

It took me nine hours to go from Taunton to Bath, before the invention of rail roads, and I now go in six hours from Taunton to London.

I can walk, by the assistance of the police, from one end of London to the other, without molestation.

I had no umbrella! There were no waterproof hats, and my hat has often been reduced by rains into pulp.

I could not keep my small clothes in their proper place, for braces were unknown. If I had the gout, there were no painkillers.

There were filthy coffee-houses instead of elegant clubs. The corruptions of Parliament, before Reform, were infamous. There were no banks to receive the savings of the poor. Whatever miseries I suffered, I had no post to whisk my complaints for a single penny to the remotest corners of the empire; and yet, in spite of all these privations, I lived on quietly, and am now ashamed that I was not more discontented.

Reverend Sydney Smith (1771–1845).

Rev Sydney Smith was a reformer, campaigning for the reform of Parliament (see Chapter 5) and for religious toleration. He saw the improvements of the Industrial Revolution era as symbolic of a deeper improvement in the nature of people.

The Victorians were excessively pleased with themselves. In 1859 the Victorian writer Samuel Smiles published *Self-Help*. His theory was that, if you are diligent, honest and careful with money, you can be successful.

The upshot of this was that rich Victorians believed that they had gained their wealth because they were in some way superior – cleverer, harder-working, more godly – than other people. In the same way, they believed that Britain was the greatest nation on earth because the British were the most powerful race on earth.

The flip-side of this was that well-to-do Victorians tended to assume that poverty was the result of some fault of character or vice (usually drink), and that foreign races were inferior (especially those which were not Christian). Economic strength, therefore, went hand in hand with **racism** and prejudice.

SOURCE D

Victorians loved to read 'Penny Dreadfuls' – cheap papers full of adventure and scandal. Some were novels (such as Isabella, a tale about a nun who disguised herself as a man and had many adventures). Others related true-life crime stories such as Jack the Ripper or 'Springheeled Jack'.

SOURCE E

A feature of Victorian society was the 'Freak Show'. One famous oddity was John Merrick, the 'Elephant Man', of whom it was said: 'women and nervous persons fly in terror from the sight of him'. He was rescued and cared for by the surgeon Sir Frederick Treves.

THINK ABOUT IT

1. What did Prince Albert (page 8) mean by the phrase: 'himself a divine instrument'?

2. The Victorians were not prone to understatement! Read Source C. Make a list of all the words that emphasise how bad things were in the past.

3. Changing words and sentence structure as necessary, rewrite Source C (or a section of it) as it would have been written by someone who *hated* the changes.

4. Make a list of all the 'marvels' mentioned on pages 7–9.

5. The Victorians were fascinated by marvels and oddities. Which aspects of this fascination, shown on these pages, would we consider *not* politically correct nowadays?

STOP AND REFLECT:

Write two paragraphs explaining how the Victorians' successes affected their attitudes to:
a. themselves
b. other people?

Concentrate on explaining the thought-processes which led them to develop these attitudes.

How did the Industrial Revolution change industry?

SOURCE Ⓐ

Ironbridge

Of the iron bridge, which we cross'd and where we stopp'd for half and hour, what shall I say? That it must be the admiration, as it is one of the wonders, of the world.

John Byng, a visitor to Ironbridge in 1781.

Iron

In 1770, most iron was produced in Kent and Sussex, using charcoal to smelt the ore. The industry was in decline – it could not get enough charcoal to keep smelting the ore.

However, the iron industry was revolutionised by a discovery made 60 years earlier by Abraham Darby I, owner of the Coalbrookdale works in Shropshire. Darby had found a way to make cast iron using coal. After 1770, ironmakers were able to produce large quantities of iron in this way.

Iron became an essential component of the Industrial Revolution. In 1781, Abraham Darby III (Darby's grandson) built the first iron bridge of cast iron. One ironmaker – 'Iron mad' Wilkinson from Shropshire – discovered how to bore cannon from cast iron, built the first iron boat (1787), built an iron chapel for his workers, and demanded to be buried in an iron coffin!

Many of the new factories were built of cast iron, and the new machines and machine parts were made of wrought iron. Iron was also used for trains, ships and tools, as well as a host of domestic items, such as fireplaces, railings, mangles and cookers.

Coal

Coal did not cause the Industrial Revolution – at first, water wheels supplied the power for industry – but the Industrial Revolution could not have happened without coal.

Coal mining was a dangerous and dirty job, but the Victorians found it fascinating and exciting. There were many descriptions of visits down mines, and pit disasters (of which there were many) grabbed the headlines. It was constantly said that 'Coal was King', and that Britain's power depended on coal.

SOURCE Ⓑ

This engraving of 16 October 1858 shows a fire at the pit at Page Bank Colliery, County Durham. The **Illustrated London News** *had an illustrator on call to rush to the scene of any disaster and record the details.*

Textiles

Before the Industrial Revolution, cloth was produced by people working on hand-spinning wheels and hand-looms in their own homes. However, a string of **innovations** in weaving and spinning revolutionised the industry. In the 20 years after 1785, manufacturers could produce spun thread 200 times faster and at a quarter of the price of the old hand-spinning wheels. Industrialists built huge factories, and bought rows of steam-powered machines to put in them.

SOURCE ⓒ

*Lister's Mill in Bradford shows the vast **investment** in textiles. For the Victorian writer Andrew Ure, Britain's factories were 'magnificent buildings, surpassing by far in number, value, usefulness, and cleverness of construction, the boasted monuments of Egyptian and Roman despotism'.*

Because the new machines needed steam engines to power the machinery, the centre of the textiles industry moved to the coalfields of the north of England.

Many historians believe that cotton was the leading industry of the Industrial Revolution. They argue that the growth of the cotton industry in the 1780s kick-started the iron industry (the factories and machines were made from iron), the coal industry (the steam engines used coal), and the building, transport and engineering industries.

FACT FILE

Key Inventions of the Industrial Revolution

1709 Abraham Darby made iron using coal.

1715 Newcomen developed a steam engine to drain the coalmines.

1733 Kay's Flying Shuttle speeded up weaving.

1765 Hargreaves' 'Spinning Jenny', followed by Arkwright's 'Water Frame' (1769) and Crompton's 'Mule' (1779), mechanised spinning.

1781 Watt's steam engine provided a source of power for industry.

1783 Henry Cort discovered a way of 'puddling' cast iron to make wrought iron.

1785 Cartwright's 'Power Loom' allowed steam-powered weaving.

1815 Safety lamps invented by Humphrey Davy and George Stephenson allowed coal to be mined in dangerous pits.

1856 Henry Bessemer and then Sidney Gilchrist-Thomas (1878) discovered ways to mass-produce steel.

THINK ABOUT IT

1. Reading pages 10–11, what would you say were the key features of the Industrial Revolution?

2. Look at Sources A–C. If you had to choose one of these as the emblem of the Industrial Revolution, which would you choose, and why?

3. Many historians believe that it was not iron, coal or textiles alone that caused the Industrial Revolution, but the three industries interacting together. Find as many examples as you can of the iron, coal and textiles industries helping each other to grow.

STOP AND REFLECT: Write a paragraph to explain what the Victorians thought about the 'revolution' in the iron, coal and textiles industries.

How did railways change the Victorians' world?

Results of the railways

Invented to haul coal in the mines of the north-east, the railways brought together all the developments of the Industrial Revolution – iron, coal, steam engines and machine engineering. The railways revolutionised trade – they could transport more goods, faster and cheaper than ever before. Raising the money to build them created our modern Stock Exchange. The vast amount of money paid out in purchases and wages stimulated other industries. Railways could take anyone anywhere in the country in less than a day and led, incidentally, to the modern habit of going to the seaside.

Trains were metal machines travelling at high speed; the mechanical engineering industry grew up to develop and repair the machines and the rails. The lines had to span gorges, bore through hills, cross marshes and flatten slums, which led to significant developments in civil engineering.

Not just the trains, but life itself, speeded up. In the past, every town had set its clocks to its own time; now, to prevent crashes and missed connections, everybody, everywhere, set their watches to 'Railway Time'. The telegraph – developed to pass messages between stations – revolutionised communications. Railways changed the world.

SOURCE Ⓐ

Rain, Steam, and Speed: The Great Western Railway (1844) by the English artist JMW Turner shows a train crossing a bridge. On the left, people sail on the river; on the right a man is ploughing.

*Through this traditional world comes the black, fiery train. One art historian calls the picture 'a celebration of our new **technological** power ... as threatening as a ghost train about to burst through your bedroom wall in the dead of night.'*

SOURCE B

W P Frith, The Railway Station *(1862), showing the Great Western Railway terminus at Paddington Station in London. Can you see:*
- *the station, the train and the carriages?*
- *a criminal being arrested?*
- *Frith in the centre of the painting, surrounded by his family?*
- *a bride and groom?*
- *a boy off to boarding school?*
- *the engine driver on the footplate of the train?*

◆ Originally, Louis Flatlow, who commissioned the painting, wanted to be shown as the engine driver, but the real driver insisted that *he* be the driver, so Flatlow had to be merely a man talking to him! Can you see Flatlow, in the brown cloak, by the train?

THINK ABOUT IT

1. What feelings does the Turner painting *Rain, Steam, and Speed* convey about the railways?

2. Imagine you are from a small country village, coming into London for the first time, and you alight from the train to the scene in Frith's *Railway Station*. With a partner, improvise a scene where you are telling your friend about what you 'saw', as though you had been there. Try to capture the Victorians' sense of awe and excitement.

STOP AND REFLECT: List all the evidence you can to show that the Victorians were amazed and delighted by the railways.

Was Brunel the 'Greatest Briton'?

In 2002, BBC2 TV held a competition to find 'The Greatest Briton'. The case for Isambard Kingdom Brunel (1806–59) was put by TV presenter Jeremy Clarkson. In the end, Winston Churchill came first with 450,000 votes, but Brunel came second with nearly 400,000 votes – almost twice the number cast for Princess Diana, and almost four times as many as for Darwin and Shakespeare!

What was so amazing about Isambard Kingdom Brunel?

1. He cut his engineering teeth (in 1823 aged 17) as engineer of the Thames Tunnel his father was building. Brunel had to overcome huge problems – on one occasion the tunnel flooded, killing ten workmen, almost drowning him, and halting work for seven years.

2. In 1829 (aged 23) Brunel designed a suspension bridge to cross the River Avon at Clifton. (Because of a lack of funds the bridge was not built until after his death.)

3. In 1831 (aged 25) Brunel designed the Monkwearmouth Docks. He later designed and built docks at other ports.

4. Entertaining his wife-to-be with a magic trick, Brunel swallowed a coin that stuck in his lungs. When a surgeon failed to retrieve the coin, Brunel invented a rocking table that turned him upside down and jiggled him. Several days later, the coin came out. The rocking table was used by surgeons in operations for many years afterwards.

5. In 1833 (aged 27) Brunel became engineer of the Great Western Railway from London to Bristol. Its design was cutting-edge. Brunel used a broad gauge (2.2m) instead of the standard gauge (1.55m) used on other lines. Although more comfortable, this created problems where the two gauges met.

6. Brunel was a workaholic who regularly worked an 18-hour day. In 1836 he took three days off for his honeymoon (which included a visit to see the Liverpool–Manchester railway).

THE LIVERPOOL AND
MANCHESTER
RAILWAY

BEWARE OF TRAINS
LOOK BOTH UP AND
DOWN THE LINE
BEFORE YOU CROSS

7. Brunel wanted a continuous passenger route from London to New York. So in 1838 he built the **Great Western** *paddle steamer*, which made its first voyage from Bristol to New York. It was 86m (236 feet) long – at the time the largest steamship ever built. In 1845, he completed the **Great Britain** steamship – powered by a screw propeller.

8. During the Crimean War (1854) he helped Florence Nightingale by designing a pre-fabricated hospital for the injured.

9. In 1852 he began to build another steamship, the **Great Eastern**, bigger than any ship ever built. This was Brunel's greatest task. There were financial and engineering problems (his design was beyond the materials available and his partner was a crook) and he was attacked in the press.

THINK ABOUT IT

1. Write an information text about Brunel, suitable for inclusion in an encyclopaedia. Remember to use:

   - clear, factual sentences
   - vocabulary of precision – dates and numbers
   - impersonal language – no value-judgement adjectives
   - bad, as well as good, things about him

2. Write a persuasion text about Brunel, as if you were a TV presenter trying to get people to vote for him. This time you can use:

   - broad, value-laden claims
   - vocabulary of description – powerful adjectives and images
   - emotive language – facts used to 'prove' claims
   - only the 'positive' things you have learned about him.

SOURCE B

Raving About Brunel

Isambard Brunel expanded engineering technique beyond anything known or imagined…

He set the mood of the technology of his century. Never before or since have we reached such glorious confidence in our ability to build all the way out to the far fringes of human imagination.

John Lienhard, from the University of Houston.

STOP AND REFLECT: Write a paragraph to answer the question: 'What was so amazing about Isambard Kingdom Brunel?'

What could you see at the Great Exhibition?

The brainchild of Prince Albert, the Great Exhibition of 1851 was designed to show the industrial and military achievements of Great Britain compared to the 'less **civilised**' countries.

It was opened on 1 May 1851 by Queen Victoria. More than six million visitors went to see it – *The Times* called it 'a fairy palace within walls of glass and iron'. At the Exhibition, 100,000 exhibits were displayed by 13,937 exhibitors.

The displays illustrated the history of art and architecture, as well as the world of industry and nature. The novelist Charlotte Brontë wrote: 'Whatever human industry has created, you will find it there'.

Concerts were held in the huge arched nave, which also housed the world's largest organ. Other attractions included a circus, tightrope-walking and the fabulous Koh-i-Noor diamond, recently acquired from India.

SOURCE Ⓐ

On entering the building for the first time, the eye is completely dazzled... We have here the Indian Court, Africa, Canada, the West Indies... Sheffield and its hardware, the woollen and mixed cloth, printing and dyeing... general hardware, brass and iron-work of all kinds, locks, grates... agricultural machines and implements... the mineral products of England... cotton and woollen power-looms in motion... rope making lathes, marine engines, hydraulic presses, steam machinery... Persia, Greece, Egypt, and Turkey, France, its tapestry, machinery, arms and instruments, occupying two large courts... and the United States, with its agricultural implements, raw materials etc...

In the British half are the silks and shawls, lace and embroideries, jewellery and clocks and watches, behind them military arms and models, chemicals, naval architecture, philosophical instruments, civil engineering, musical instruments, anatomical models, glass chandeliers, china, cutlery, and animal and vegetable manufactures, china and pottery... on the opposite side perfumery, toys, fishing materials, wax flowers and stained glass.

The Art Journal *(1851).*

SOURCE Ⓑ

The Great Exhibition was held in Hyde Park in London in the specially built Crystal Palace – a huge frame of iron with 293,655 panes of glass. The building covered 19 acres. The main nave was 674 metres (1,848 feet) long and 149 metres (408 feet) wide.

The Main Nave (note the use of a Church word to describe the building).

No Sunday opening was allowed, no alcohol, no smoking and no dogs. Schweppes paid £5500 for the contract to provide refreshments, and sold 1,092,337 bottles of soft drinks.

SOURCE D

The Exhibition displayed British prejudice as well as British achievements. In this cartoon, 'cannibal islanders' at the restaurant are shown looking with great interest at a visiting couple's young son.

THINK ABOUT IT

1. Using Source A, list all the different countries it mentions. Why do you think it was so important to the Victorians that all these countries were represented?

2. The Great Exhibition had a huge impact on the people who saw it: 'It's magical, intoxicating, a spectacle such as the world will scarcely see again'. Why, do you think, did the Great Exhibition have such a great impact on the Victorians?

3. How was the Great Exhibition 'a natural and inevitable product of the Industrial Revolution'?

STOP AND REFLECT: Use pages 16–17 to make a list of things you might have seen at the Great Exhibition (there are at least 40).

Pulling it Together

How did the Victorians feel about the Industrial Revolution?

The theme of this chapter has been that the Victorians were amazed by their world – not just the advances and achievements of industry, but the wonders of nature and the heights (and the depths) of human achievement. The Victorians constantly wanted to be astounded – or horrified. One of the ideas in Chapter 2 will be that maybe this Victorian fascination with sensation has given us a wrong impression of the times.

Stage 1 Preparation

1. Working with a partner, using pages 7–17, make a list of all the words associated with 'amazement'.
2. Gather your notes from pages 4–15 on the marvels of the Victorian age, and especially *the attitude of the Victorians to them.*
3. Consult your list of things to see at the Great Exhibition.

Stage 2 Writing the letter

You are going to imagine that you are a Victorian who visited the Great Exhibition. Write a letter to a friend about what you 'saw'.
● You will write in the first person, past tense.

This could be a simple recount of what you 'saw'. Better assignments, however, will contain elements of evaluation, analysis and persuasion, so you will need to:
● use connectives for contrast and comparison in areas of debate, words such as *though, while, equally, also* (e.g. 'although I did like the…, I also enjoyed…')

● use evidence to support the claims you are making (e.g. 'This was wonderful because…').

● use imagery in your description, especially metaphors and similes.

● include value judgements, comment and reflection, using phrases such as 'I felt that…', 'It seemed as if…', seeking to influence your reader's reaction.

(a) The basic letter will describe the sights and sounds of the Exhibition.

(b) A better letter will include authentic-sounding statements of enthusiasm and amazement.

(c) The very good letter will link the exhibits at the Great Exhibition to what you know about the developments in textiles, iron, coal and railways, and to Victorian society and culture.

(d) The best letter will include authentic-sounding Victorian attitudes about what you are describing.

CHAPTER 2

A Case of Murder
Did the Industrial Revolution destroy its own children?

In this chapter you will:

- Consider whether the Victorians ruined the environment.
- Discuss whether workers were badly treated during the Industrial Revolution.
- Learn about the 'model village' of Saltaire.
- Study the growth of trade unions in the nineteenth century.
- Debate whether the Industrial Revolution oppressed and caused the death of many people.

In 1847 Frederick Engels, a young German whose father owned a factory in Manchester, attended the Congress of the **Communist** League in London. Engels had been horrified by the conditions of the people of Manchester, and now he put forward his ideas.

Engels blamed the suffering of the workers on the inventions of the Industrial Revolution, which had made them 'servants of the machine', doing monotonous work for the lowest wage possible. They had become 'wage-slaves', a state worse than even the slavery of old, said Engels.

SOURCE A

Crushing the Workers
In this George Cruickshank cartoon, an evil factory owner runs his factory (symbolised by the mincing machine).

But how true is all this? In fact, many Victorians were caring people who accepted that the government had a duty to care for its citizens (see the Fact File). Much of our evidence about the bad conditions comes from investigations set up by Parliament, so that laws could be put in place to improve things. The Victorians were terribly melodramatic about the sufferings of the poor. Have historians been fooled by their exaggerations, and come to the conclusion that things were worse than they really were?

It is often said of political revolutions (such as the French Revolution) that they end up 'devouring their own children' (that is, executing the people who started the revolution). Is this also true of the Industrial Revolution? It is indisputable that many people died in the factories and mines of Victorian England.

Yet were the Victorians to blame? In the Court of Human History, should we find the Victorians guilty of murder, or merely of manslaughter (unintentional killing)? Or might we decide that they were innocent – that, if people died, it was not the Victorians' fault?

SOURCE Ⓑ

It is well to remember that the Industrial Revolution created the wealth that we enjoy today and that the Industrial Revolution was paid for in the blood of workers — men, women, and children.

Lynn H Nelson, **The Second Industrial Revolution (1998).**

FACT FILE
Victorian Reforms

1824 The Combinations Act allowed **Trade Unions** to exist.

1833 The Factories Act improved conditions for children in factories.

1842 The Mines Act improved conditions for women and children in mines.

1847 The Ten Hours Act limited women and children to a 58-hour week.

1875 The Conspiracy Act allowed peaceful **picketing**.

1908 Pensions for old people over 70.

1911 Sick pay for workers who were ill.

THINK ABOUT IT

1. Describe what you can see in Source A.

2. The intention of the cartoon is *persuasion* – to convince the viewer that the factory system is cruel. What are the three key points of the cartoonist case?

3. Now present the message of the cartoon as a written persuasive text.

   ● Use a paragraph for each key point.

   ● Present each point as a statement and then elaboration.

   ● Use 'value-judgement words' to influence the reader.

   ● Use logic connectives such as 'because' and 'therefore'.

   ● Finish with a conclusion: 'Therefore, it is clear that factories…'

Did the Victorians ruin the environment?

SOURCE Ⓐ

A painting by Philip de Loutherbourg showing the Bedlam iron furnace at Coalbrookdale. An Italian, visiting in 1787, wrote: 'The approach appeared to be a veritable descent to hell'.

It is indisputable that the Industrial Revolution damaged the environment. Nineteenth-century industry scarred the landscape and polluted the air and rivers.

SOURCE Ⓑ

The Iron Industry at Coalbrookdale

O violated Coalbrook!

Amid thy grassy lanes, thy woodwild glens,

Thy knolls and bubbling wells, thy rocks, and streams,

– Now we hear, in mingled tones,

Shout their throng'd barge, their pond'rous engines clang

Through the coy dales; while red the countless fires,

With black flames, bicker on all the hills,

Dark'ning the Summer's sun with columns large

Of thick, sulphureous smoke, which spread, like palls,

That pollute thy gales, and stain thy glassy water.

A poem written by Anna Seward (1785).

THINK ABOUT IT

1. **Study Source B.**

    List the value-judgement words the poet uses to describe the dale before and after industrialisation. How does her use of words show her feelings?

2. **Which is of more use to an historian studying the impact of the iron industry on the environment – Source A or Source B?**

SOURCE C

The 'Black Country', in the Midlands, in the mid-nineteenth century. Throughout the industrial north, the steam engines and factories spewed out smoke. If it turned the buildings black, what was it doing to people's lungs? There was immediate damage to workers' health, and there were long-term consequences for today. Scientists blame the global warming of today on the huge quantities of smoke emitted during industrialisation.

SOURCE D

Lead poisoning of lead miners

A healthy young man enters upon work in a lead mine; in a few years he is 'touched in the wind'. Along with this there is an increased spitting of mucus, often tinged, especially after leaving work, of a bluish black colour. His appetite for food is reduced, and what he takes for breakfast is frequently vomited as he walks to work. He has great languor, and frequently fits of severe coughing… He may now be up to 40 or 45 years of age; he is low in health and strength, and compelled to give up work. He may wander about for some years, but… the poor worn-out miner now soon dies exhausted.

> *Dr Ewart (surgeon to the London Lead Company), giving evidence to the Royal Commission on the Mines (1864).*

♦ *The effects of lead poisoning were so severe that, in 1858, the lead-mining town of Alston had more widows than any other place in Britain.*

♦ *Other industries had occupational diseases, for instance the textiles industry, the coal mining industry, and the match-making industry.*

Even at the time many people were questioning what was happening. The poet William Wordsworth was one of the campaigners who hated industrialisation, and he tried unsuccessfully to stop the Kendal to Windermere railway invading the Lake District.

SOURCE E

Bradford Canal in 1844

The drains of the town are emptied into the canal. Besides, on the sides of the stream there are a great many factories, the soil, refuse and filth of which fall into the water… The millowners, having a deficiency of water, contract with the owners of the canal for a supply of water to their boilers. After being used for the generation of steam, the water is conveyed back into the canal, so that the waters of the canal are scarcely ever cool, and constantly emit the most offensive gases.

> *William Cudworth, Bradford Corporation (1881).*

♦ *Damage was also done to the rivers by the iron and chemicals industries.*

SOURCE F

All over the coalfields, mines left huge pit heaps, like this one at Aberfan, in Wales, which collapsed on 21 October 1966. A total of 144 people were killed, 116 of them children, who were at school when it was engulfed. The Industrial Revolution did not only kill its own children.

SOURCE G

Britain was damaged

When the UK was industrialising, the effects of pollution were not understood... In consequence, the environment of Britain was damaged, and generations suffered from the effects of poor air and water, noise, and dirt... Industrial wastes were dumped into water courses, and the air became polluted from **emissions**. During the nineteenth century, municipal authorities realised that something had to be done about pollution.

British Council Briefing Sheet, The UK Environmental Industry *(1999).*

FACT FILE

Victorians' laws against pollution

1848 Nuisances Removal Act

1853 Smoke Nuisance **Abatement** Act

1863 Alkali Act (to stop chemical pollution)

1865 Sewerage Act

1876 River Pollution Act

1897 **Public Health** stated 'of all the achievements of the Victorian Era... history will find none worthier than the efforts... to secure for all pure air, food, and water'.

THINK ABOUT IT

1. How is the Industrial Revolution still harming us, today?

2. If the Victorians did not know about the effects of pollution (Source G), can they be blamed for it?

3. If the Victorians took steps to try to protect the environment (see Fact File), can we accuse them of *murdering* people?

4. Can you think of any examples from the present day where companies or institutions have acted in a way that has led to death or suffering, or where our trade or lifestyle is damaging the environment? Consider the idea that it is sheer hypocrisy for the modern age to accuse the Victorians.

STOP AND REFLECT: Write four paragraphs on nineteenth-century pollution under the heads: 'air', 'water', 'landscape', and 'occupational diseases'.

Was there 'child-slavery' in the nineteenth century?

In 1830, a Yorkshireman named Richard Oastler wrote to the *Leeds Mercury* claiming that the factory system in Yorkshire was more cruel to children than the system of slavery in the West Indies.

The two enquiries on pages 24–29 ask whether he was justified in making this claim.

SOURCE A

Factory children in the nineteenth century.

SOURCE B

What historians have said about the Sadler Report

It is one of the main sources of our knowledge of the kind of life that was led by the victims of the new system.

J L and B Hammond, **Lord Shaftesbury** *(1923)*.

It is one of the most valuable collections of evidence on industrial conditions that we possess.

B L Hutchins and A Harrison, **A History of Factory Legislation** *(1966)*.

By far the most-used source on factory children is a Parliamentary Report of 1832 by the MP Michael Sadler. Sadler interviewed dozens of people, including mill owners, overseers, parents and workers. His report gives a vivid impression of life for factory children.

Working in a factory

A child's day began at 4 a.m. Such was the terror of being late to work that some parents stayed awake all night to make sure they got their children up in time. They often had to shake their children to wake them up.

Few men worked – children were cheaper to employ. Parents interviewed by Sadler said they would prefer their children not to go to the factory, but admitted that 'necessity compels a man with children to let them work'. So the children had to hurry to the factory – sometimes two miles away. Few had time for breakfast. One witness said: 'I have seen children running down to the mill crying, a bit of bread in their hand, and that is all they have till 12 noon'.

Those who were half a minute late were fined, and it was not unknown for the overlookers (the foremen) to alter the clock to make sure they were. Workers were fined for many reasons – combing their hair, speaking, leaving a window open, and so on. Overlookers who did not get large sums in fines were sacked.

Children started factory work as young as six, and usually at seven or eight years of age. They were rarely allowed to sit down, and frequently grew up with twisted spines, hunched shoulders, knock knees or bow legs.

SOURCE C

An illustration from the novel Michael Armstrong, Factory Boy (1840). Note the girl 'scavenger' sweeping up the cotton dust underneath the spinning machine, and the 'pieceners', whose job was to lean into the machinery and tie the threads that broke.

Inside the cotton mill it was hot and damp (to stop the threads from snapping). The machinery was deafeningly noisy, and the air thick with cotton dust, so many workers developed lung diseases. The fibres got into the children's food, and upset their appetite.

A normal working day was 14 hours, with half an hour for lunch. According to one witness, in the six-week 'brisk' (busy) time the working day for his children started at 3 a.m. and finished at 10.30 at night; an amazing $19\frac{1}{2}$ hour day. Some mills made the workers 'dry down' (clean) the machines in their meal-break.

As the day went on, the children became tired and the overlookers had to force them to keep pace with the machines. 'Strapping' was usual, but overlookers were also said to dip children into tubs of water, gag them and shake them. Extreme punishments included an iron rod pushed through a girl's cheek, and a child thrashed to death.

One witness told Sadler that there was never an hour when you could be in a mill without hearing a child crying.

In the days before safety guards on machinery became law, it was dangerous work, especially towards the end of the day when the children became weary. Accidents reported to the committee included a man caught up by the drive belt and killed, and a girl who had her finger twisted off by a cog.

Getting home late at night, tired, children simply went to bed without eating, or fell asleep with the food in their mouths. By now, it might be midnight, and they had to be up at 4 a.m. the next morning, to go through it all over again. One witness, Matthew Crabtree, remembered: 'I used to cry all the way as I went to the mill'.

THINK ABOUT IT

Study Source C.

How does the artist create an atmosphere of misery and cruelty?

SOURCE ⓓ

Interview with a factory child

At what age did you commence work? Seven years of age.

What was the employment? Spinning.

What were your hours of labour at that mill? From five in the morning till eight at night.

What intervals had you for refreshment and rest? Thirty minutes at noon.

Had you no time for breakfast or refreshment in the afternoon? No, not one minute; we had to eat our meals as we could, standing.

You had 14 $\frac{1}{2}$ hours of actual labour at seven years of age? Yes.

What effect had this labour upon your own health? When I had worked about half a year, a weakness fell into my knees and ankles; it continued, and it has got worse and worse.

Was it painful for you to move? Yes, in the morning I could scarcely walk, and my brother and sister used, out of kindness, to take me under each arm, and run with me to the mill, and my legs dragged on the ground; in consequence of the pain I could not walk.

Were you sometimes late? Yes; and if we were five minutes late, the overlooker would take a strap, and beat us till we were black and blue.

Was the main business of one of the overlookers that of strapping the children up to this excessive labour? Yes, he is continually walking up and down with it in his hand.

Have any cases of accidents in mills or factories been brought into the Infirmary since you were there? Yes, last Tuesday but one there was a boy brought in about five or six o'clock in the evening from a mill; he had got catched with a shaft, and he had both his thighs broke, and from his knee to his hip the flesh was ripped up the same as if it had been cut by a knife, his head was bruised, his eyes were nearly torn out, and his arms broken.

Sadler Report, 1832: evidence of Joseph Hebergam

THINK ABOUT IT

1. Study and discuss Joseph Hebergam's interview with Sadler (Source D). Make a list of all the facts it gives about his work in the factory.

2. Using all the information on pages 24–26, work with a partner to devise a set of questions and answers for an imaginary child-worker, to imitate the actual interview of Joseph Hebergam.

3. Do you think the system of child labour in Britain's factories was 'more horrid than slavery'?

4. Is there any comparison between the working conditions of children in nineteenth-century Britain and those in some less economically developed countries today?

STOP AND REFLECT:
Write a paragraph identifying and commenting on the elements that made factory work so horrid for children.

Was Sadler correct?

We have already suggested (page 20) that maybe the Victorians' desire to sensationalise has given us a wrong impression of the times. Was this true of the Sadler report?

Some writers, however, accuse Sadler of worse even than this. Did he lie, lead witnesses and falsify the results?

SOURCE F

Interview with a factory child's father

At what time in the morning, in the brisk time, did those girls go to the mill? In the brisk time, for about six weeks, they have gone at three o'clock in the morning, and ended at ten, or nearly half-past, at night.

What intervals were allowed for rest or refreshment during those nineteen hours of labour? Breakfast a quarter of an hour, and dinner half an hour, and drinking a quarter of an hour.

What was the length of time they could be in bed during those long hours? It was near eleven o'clock before we could get them into bed after getting a little food, and then at morning my mistress used to stop up all night, for fear that we could not get them ready for the time.

What time did you get them up in the morning? Me or my mistress got up at two o'clock to dress them.

So that they had not above four hours' sleep at this time? No, they had not.

Were the children excessively fatigued by this labour? Many times; we have cried often when we have given them the little food we had to give them; we had to shake them, and they have fallen to sleep with the food in their mouths many a time.

Did this excessive term of labour occasion much cruelty also? Yes, with being so very much fatigued the strap was very frequently used.

Sadler Report, 1832: evidence of Samuel Coulson

SOURCE E

A picture in a textbook, The Progress of Cotton *(1835). Historians suggest the illustrator of* Michael Armstrong, Factory Boy *(Source C) used this as the basis for his picture.*

THINK ABOUT IT

1. Look at the evidence of Samuel Coulson (Source F). What answers seem to you to be exaggerated/playing for sympathy?

2. Study Hebergam's testimony (Source D on page 26) in the same way. Do any of Hebergam's answers seem exaggerated or playing for sympathy?

3. Study Sources C (on page 25) and E. Have you any reason to think Source C is *not* a true representation of factory life?

SOURCE G

Sadler had been agitating for factory reform, and in doing so he employed every cheap political trick in the book, including the falsification of evidence.

Lawrence W Reed, Child Labor and the British Industrial Revolution *(1991).*

◆ *Reed is a modern economist, who advocates that industry should not be too greatly regulated by laws.*

SOURCE H

Such a mass of **biased** statements, and of gross falsehoods and lies... as probably never before found their way into any public document.

Robert Hyde Greg, The Factory Question *(1837).*

◆ *Greg was a factory owner who employed children.*

SOURCE I

This is a very biased document, drawn up entirely by enemies of the factory system for purely political purposes. Sadler was led astray by his passionate sympathies into making assertions of a most misleading and erroneous kind. He asked witnesses questions in such a way as to produce answers which, although correct, nevertheless were stated in such a form as to give a wholly false impression.

Frederick Engels, The Condition of the Working Classes in England *(1844).*

◆ *Engels was a Communist.*

Michael Sadler was the leader of the campaign to improve conditions for factory children. In 1832, however, he lost his seat in Parliament, and Lord Ashley (later to become Lord Shaftesbury) took over leadership of the movement. In 1833, Ashley chaired a **Royal Commission** on factory conditions.

The Commission found that children worked long hours, and that laws were needed to protect them. It also found, however, that some of the evidence given to the Sadler committee had been exaggerated. For instance, Joseph Hebergam – who had claimed that he had frequent accidents at work – admitted to the commission that 'the accidents I meant were hurting my knuckles. I can't recollect that I ever saw anything worse than that'.

THINK ABOUT IT

1. Look at Sources G–I.
   Which do you think is the most reliable? Why?
2. Engels (Source I) accuses Sadler of asking 'leading' questions (i.e. that he 'put words into their mouths').
   Find examples of leading questions in Sources D and F.

SOURCE J

After 1833, the government appointed factory inspectors to make sure that child-workers were correctly treated. This late nineteenth-century illustration is from the **London Illustrated News.**

Many writers and illustrators in the nineteenth century were insistent that factory work was not, *in itself,* oppressive, that it was not even tiring, and that it was far better than the alternative – starving to death on the streets.

SOURCE L

Places of leisure

In the factory, the driving force of the machinery leaves the attendant nearly nothing at all to do. It was delightful to observe the children's nimbleness...and to see them at leisure, after a few seconds' exercise of their tiny fingers... I never saw a single instance of corporal punishment inflicted on a child. The children seemed to be always cheerful and alert... As to exhaustion by the day's work, they showed no trace of it on leaving the mill in the evening; for they immediately began to skip about any neighbouring playground.

Andrew Ure, **The Philosophy of Manufactures (1835).**

SOURCE K

A girl working in a lace factory near Nottingham, 1884. By this date, she would have been working 'half-time', and going to school for the rest of the day.

THINK ABOUT IT

1. Look at the pictures on pages 27–29.

   How do they differ from those on pages 24–25? Which do you think are nearest to the truth?

2. What impression do Sources J–L give of work in factories?

3. Ask your teacher to lead a class discussion:

   'Was Sadler telling the truth?'

STOP AND REFLECT: Write a paragraph summing up the reasons why we might not rely on the information provided in Sadler's Report.

How was Saltaire a 'model village'?

By the 1840s the woollen town of Bradford was: 'over-crowded, dirty, and smoky, a stink of filth, pollution, and foul diseases'. One mill owner, Titus Salt, wanted better for his 3000 workers, so he built a mill and a model village beside the River Aire, four miles outside Bradford 'in the midst the most beautiful scenery'.

Salt named his model village Saltaire. He did not oppose child labour, he believed that the poor should work hard for their living. But he was a kind and dedicated Christian who believed it was his duty to use his wealth to provide his workers with a pleasant environment, education and space to play.

(a) The Mill, opened in 1853, had cast-iron pillars supporting an iron roof, and housed 1200 looms. The chimney was built 68 metres (250 feet) high to reduce smoke pollution.

(b) The workmen's houses were well built and rented cheaply. Every street had a back alley, so soil could be taken from the privies without going through the house. The houses were not overcrowded, and many wives did not go out to work.

(c) In 1854 Salt built a Mill dining room where the workers could buy a cheap, good breakfast and lunch. Salt also built shops, a bathhouse and a washhouse, and provided his workers with allotments.

*(d) Salt built 45 one-bedroomed **almshouses** for workers who were unable to work due to old age or illness. Each received a pension of 7s 6d a week, and lived in the almshouse rent-free.*

(e) In 1868 Salt opened a six-bed cottage hospital for the workers and their families. Salt's workers contributed to an insurance fund, which paid them a small sickness benefit if they became ill.

(f) Salt built a school (1868) for 700 workers' children, many of whom worked half-time at the Mill. One of its pupils went on to be a Professor at Oxford University.

(g) The Victoria Hall Institute (1871) housed a library, chess rooms, smoking room, billiard tables, a lecture hall, a gym, Schools of Art and Science, and a drill room for the local Rifle Volunteers.

(h) Facing the Mill, in 1859, Salt built a magnificent Congregational Chapel, costing £16,000. He also spent £7000 on a Sunday School that had 22 rooms and 800 pupils.

THINK ABOUT IT

Using the materials on pages 30-31, prepare an imaginary 'guided tour' round Saltaire.

Write this as an Information text:

- Start with an introductory opening statement about Titus Salt and what he was trying to do.

- Use sub-headings to divide up the information.

- Use second person future tense when addressing the reader *(e.g. 'If you go…you will see…)*. You will have to use third person past tense when talking about Salt *(e.g. 'Here, he built…).*

- Concentrate on factual information and clarity of description.

- As this will be a promotional leaflet for tourists, use adjectives which advertise how remarkable were Saltaire and its founder.

STOP AND REFLECT: List examples where Salt was acting as a 'paternalistic' employer, treating his workers like a father would his children.

(i) Larger houses along Albert Road were built in 1866 for the foremen and overseers, the minister of the Congregational Church, the two school teachers and the company's chief cashier.

(j) In 1871, Salt opened Roberts Park. It had beautiful gardens with a cricket ground, boathouse, refreshment rooms, and a bandstand. Spitting, smoking, gambling, drunks, unaccompanied children and bad language were all forbidden.

How oppressed were workers in the nineteenth century?

Trade unions seek good wages and conditions for their workers. Except for a few people in essential services, everybody in Britain today has the right to be a member of a union.

This, however, has not always been the case. The Combination Act of 1799 forbade workers to form a trade union. Even after 1824, when Parliament repealed the Combination Acts, workers found it hard to form trade unions. The Grand National Consolidated Trade Union, formed in 1834, had half a million members, but collapsed after only a few months.

The Tolpuddle Martyrs. Loveless is bottom right.

SOURCE Ⓐ

The greater part of the evidence against us was put into the mouths of the witnesses by the judge... He told the jury that if such societies were allowed to exist, it would ruin masters, damage trade, and destroy property.

George Loveless, **Victims of Whiggery** *(1839).*

The Tolpuddle Martyrs

George Loveless was a farm labourer and Methodist preacher in Dorset. When the local farmers reduced their wages from nine shillings to only six shillings a week, he and five other local men set up a union. They met under a village tree and swore never to reveal anything of the union they had formed.

The union frightened a local landowner and magistrate named James Frampton. In March 1834 the six were put on trial for conspiracy, under an Act of 1797 to stop mutiny amongst sailors (this Act made it illegal to swear an **oath**). A local labourer called Edward Legg gave evidence that the six men had made him take an oath, a jury of local landowners (including Frampton, his son and his step-brother) found them guilty, and the judge sentenced them to be **transported** to Australia for seven years.

There was an outcry. Thousands of people petitioned against the punishment, and the government was forced to revoke the sentences and allow the 'Tolpuddle Martyrs' to return to Britain in 1838.

Progress and failure

The first successful unions were set up in the 1850s, and in 1875, the *Conspiracy and Protection of Property Act* allowed peaceful picketing, so that striking workers could try to persuade other workers to stay out with them. Even so, the 'new model unions' (as they were called) were mainly for skilled workers, and they rarely went on strike. For the unskilled masses, there was nothing.

The match-girls' strike

In June 1888, a journalist called Annie Besant wrote an article complaining about the Bryant & May match factory. Although the factory made a huge profit, it paid some of its workers as little as four shillings a week, and had a system of fines to reduce the wages even further. The factory used yellow phosphorus to make the matches, even though it was known that this caused cancer of the face, known as 'Phossy jaw'.

Soon after the article was published, Bryant & May sacked the three girls they suspected of talking to Annie Besant. Then they ordered every employee to sign a certificate stating that they treated the workers well. When some of the girls refused, their leader was sacked.

All 1400 girls went on strike. They asked Annie Besant to be their leader. They formed a union and ran a newspaper campaign urging the public not to buy Bryant & May matches. Three weeks later, the firm gave way. It re-instated the sacked girls, and ended the system of fines.

The match-girls' success stimulated the formation of trade unions for unskilled workers including, in 1889, a gas-workers' union (which today is called the GMB) and a dockers' union (today it is called the TGWU). On May Day 1890, there was a massive trade union demonstration in London. Frederick Engels was there and wrote, 'The English working class has roused itself from hibernation.'

Bryant & May match-girls on strike.

THINK ABOUT IT

1. Use the information on pages 32–33 to draw up a Fact File (like that on page 20) about the trade unions.

2. Imagine you are either George Loveless or James Frampton, or Annie Besant or Mr Bryant. Draw up a 'position paper' stating your case:

   - Start with a general statement about the situation and where you stand.
   - Be biased.

   You will want to comment on:

   - The beliefs and actions of your opponents.
   - Your own beliefs and situation.
   - The problems for the future if you lose.

STOP AND REFLECT: Look at the stories of the Tolpuddle Martyrs and the match-girls. Write a paragraph about whether the stories prove that workers were oppressed, or that their position improved, during the Industrial Revolution.

Pulling it Together

Did the Industrial Revolution destroy its own children?

The theme of this chapter has been to investigate Engels' claim that the Industrial Revolution by its nature oppressed (and killed) the workers. Some of the evidence has supported that claim. Some things you have learned suggest it is not entirely true. Sometimes, you have been asked to consider whether the evidence offered is reliable.

This assignment is set in a court of 'law', where The Industrial Revolution is in the dock charged with Murder, and your task will be to organise a case for either the prosecution (who will try to prove that it did kill the workers), or the defence (who will try to argue that it was manslaughter or less).

Stage 1 Preparation

1. You will need to be thoroughly familiar with all the information in this chapter.

2. Divide into groups of five or six, some for the 'prosecution', some for the 'defence'.

3. Each group goes through pages 19–33, building a list of the names of witnesses they are going to call to give evidence (for instance, a prosecution group might decide to call Samuel Coulson, from page 27). They then will make up a list of questions they intend to ask the witnesses, together with the answers the witnesses would give (for instance, the prosecution might ask Coulson: 'What were conditions like for your children?' and his answer would include a description of their hours and punishments).

4. At this point, teams might want to swap their lists of witnesses and questions, so that they could see if they wanted to ask any questions to 'cross-examine' the witnesses (for instance, the defence might like to quiz Samuel Coulson about whether he was exaggerating).

Stage 2 The task

With the teacher as the 'judge', the class will hold a 'court of law' to decide whether the Industrial Revolution is guilty of murder. Pupils will take the role of individual 'witnesses' and rehearse the answers they will give. Prosecution lawyers, then defence lawyers, will call witnesses, ask them the prepared questions, and cross-examine them if necessary. Then the teacher will decide which side has won, and give grades based on the quality of argument:

(a) The basic case *will call witnesses and ask questions to show whether things were bad (prosecution) or good (defence).*

(b) A better case *will call appropriate witnesses, who will give detailed answers.*

(c) The very good case *will explain as it goes along why/how this evidence proves the Industrial Revolution was (prosecution) or was not (defence) guilty of 'murder'.*

(d) The best case *will question/establish the reliability of the witnesses in order to build an argument.*

CHAPTER 3

A Tale of Two Cities

What was life like in Dickens' London?

In this chapter you will:

- Learn how Dickens wrote about London.
- Write a description of London in the time of Dickens.

SOURCE Ⓐ

Tissot's painting **London Visitors** *shows sightseers outside the National Gallery, with St Martin-in-the-Fields Church behind them. The clock reads 10:35 a.m. Boys from Christ's Hospital 'Bluecoat School' act as guides.*

The nineteenth century was a time of great civic pride, as towns vied with each other to build, not only the finest town halls, parks, libraries and museums, but also the best swimming baths, sewers and reservoirs. Councils cleaned streets, installed street lighting and set up **dispensaries**, fire brigades and tram systems.

Yet behind the façade were the filthy courts and foul hovels in which the poor were forced to live. If you went back in time and visited the poorest areas of London, the sights and smells would probably have made you physically sick.

The future Prime Minister, Benjamin Disraeli, in his novel *Sybil* (1845) wrote that there were in England 'two nations' (rich and poor) living in the same country, but utterly ignorant of each other. Dickens' novels, and the pictures in this chapter, echo Disraeli's vision of two worlds – prosperity and poverty, beauty and horror – existing side-by-side.

In this chapter you are going to consider what you might have seen if you had visited Dickens' London.

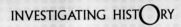

How did Charles Dickens write about London?

This Doré engraving, *Over London by Rail*, shows the housing of the poor. By 1870 there were nearly four million people living in London. The city had 300,000 houses. The city's poor lived in slums of the most unbelievable **squalor**, with problems such as lack of clean water, lack of **privies** (toilets), overflowing drains, and huge '**middens**' (muck-heaps) of decaying animal and human waste. In many parts of the city raw sewage flowed in the gutters, and outbreaks of cholera were common.

Well-off visitors to the poorer areas of London were advised first to inform the police, then to dress in rags, and finally to take two strong men to act as bodyguards.

SOURCE B

Dickens' description of a Whitechapel slum – 'Seven Dials'

The stranger who finds himself in 'The Dials' for the first time will see enough around him to keep his curiosity and attention awake for no inconsiderable time. From the irregular square into which he has plunged, the streets and courts dart in all directions, until they are lost in the unwholesome vapour which hangs over the house-tops, and renders the dirty perspective uncertain and confined. And lounging at every corner, as if they came there to take a few gasps of such fresh air as has found its way so far, but is too much exhausted already to be enabled to force itself into the narrow alleys around, are groups of people, whose appearance and dwellings would fill any mind but a regular Londoner's with astonishment…

He traverses streets of dirty, straggling houses, with now and then an unexpected court composed of buildings as ill-proportioned and deformed as the half-naked children that wallow in the gutters. Here and there, a low dingy public-house; long rows of broken and patched windows expose plants that may have flourished when 'the Dials' were built, in vessels as dirty as 'the Dials' themselves; and shops for the purchase of rags, bones, old iron, and kitchen-stuff, vie in cleanliness with the bird-fanciers and rabbit-dealers. Brokers' shops, which would seem to have been established by humane individuals, as refuges for destitute bugs, interspersed with announcements of day-schools, penny theatres, petition-writers, mangles, and music for balls; and dirty men, filthy women, squalid children, bad fruit, more than doubtful oysters, attenuated cats, depressed dogs, and anatomical fowls, are its cheerful accompaniments.

Charles Dickens, Scenes and Characters No.1 in Bell's Life in London (September 1835).

Dickens loved to describe the world in great detail. He piled up words, making long lists of details, often repeating the same connecting phrase again and again to give his passages urgency. This was partly because many of his books were written in serial form, an episode a week, for which he was paid so much a word. He loved adjectives, often describing things in new and imaginative ways.

After he became famous, Dickens gave readings of his books to ladies' literary groups. So his writing was sentimental, designed to tug the heart-strings of wealthy women. His books were also designed to be read out loud, and the words have a rhythm that sometimes makes them sound more like poetry than prose.

Dickens is famous for his use of metaphor and simile. His descriptions, often present people, their surroundings and even the weather in ways that mirror each other, so that a certain 'feel' is built up and reinforced through the passage.

SOURCE C

Dickens' description of poor London women at Covent Garden

Such stale vapid rejected cabbage-leaf and cabbage-stalk dress, such damaged-orange countenance, such squashed pulp of humanity, are open to the day nowhere else.

Charles Dickens, Our Mutual Friend *(1865).*

SOURCE D

Dickens' description of a boat ride on the River Thames

[We sailed] among the tiers of shipping, in and out, avoiding rusty chain-cables, frayed hempen hawsers and bobbing buoys, scattering floating chips of wood and shaving, cleaving floating scum of coal, in and out, hammers going in ship-builders' yards, saws going at timber, clashing engines going at things unknown, pumps going in leaky ships, ships going out to sea, and unintelligible sea-creatures roaring curses, in and out….

Charles Dickens, Great Expectations *(1861).*

THINK ABOUT IT

1. Read Sources B–D two or three times each. Can you find examples in the Sources where Dickens:

   - makes a long list of details
   - repeats the same connecting phrase again and again
   - uses more than one adjective to describe something or someone
   - uses adjectives you have not met before
   - gets sentimental about the sufferings of the poor.

2. Study Source B. Explain how Dickens describes the people, the place and the air in the same way. What effect does he thus create for the reader?

STOP AND REFLECT: 'His words have a rhythm that sometimes makes them sound like poetry.' From Sources B–D, find a particularly pleasant-sounding and rhythmic passage, and practise reading it out loud with a friend.

What might a tourist see in Dickens' London?

Sources E–J show scenes of London life about 1870. You will need to study them to do the assessment assignment on page 42.

SOURCE ⓔ

The Bayswater Omnibus by George W Joy. Notice rich and poor sharing the same bus, and the look on the face of the woman with the red umbrella. By 1900 there were 3000 horse-drawn buses in London, carrying 500 million passengers a year. Dickens believed that 'there is nothing like an omnibus', and he was fascinated by the different people who got on and off, and where they might have come from, and where they might be going.

SOURCE F *A trip to London wouldn't be the same without a visit to St James' Park and Buckingham Palace. Buckingham Palace had become the monarch's official London home when Queen Victoria moved there in 1837, though Dickens did not think it grand enough to be the royal residence. In Dickens' time, it was possible to make arrangements to see the Royal Stables and the gardens at Buckingham Palace.*

SOURCE G

This engraving of Ludgate Hill, 1870, by Gustav Doré, gives an idea of what a busy London Street was like. A traffic survey of 1850 counted 1000 vehicles an hour passing in some London streets, and traffic gridlock was a common feature of Victorian London. Street vendors selling their wares, pick-pockets, prostitutes, drunks and beggars added to the noise and the bustle. Dickens was thrilled by 'the throbbing currents' of the city's traffic which 'rushed and returned incessantly like its life's blood'. In Dickens' time, London had some 50,000 horses, which produced half a million tons of manure a year.

SOURCE H

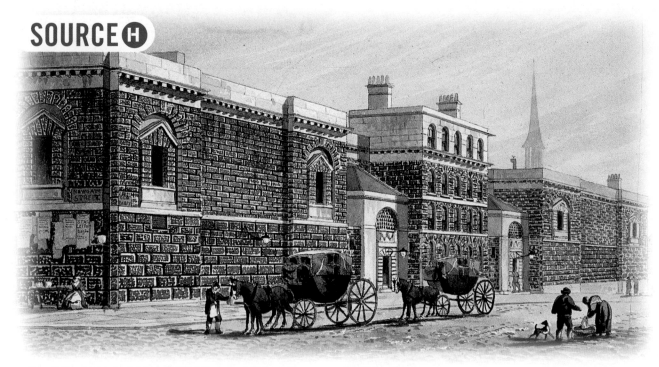

Newgate prison. There were public hangings at the prison – at which people paid for seats – until 1868. Dickens visited the prison in 1836, and was horrified by the endless doors and locks, and the lack of love between the prisoners and their visitors. As a child, Dickens had been made to go to work in a boot polish factory when his father was sent to prison for debt.

SOURCE I

Terrified that the poor might take the opportunity of getting something for nothing, the New Poor Law of 1834 had introduced the principle of '**less eligibility**' – that life on poor support had to be worse than the worst job. All relief had to be provided in the workhouse, where the inmates had to break rocks or pick oakum (unravel ropes). In this painting, poor people are waiting outside the workhouse for somewhere to stay the night.

SOURCE J

The main social season was in spring and summer, when rich people moved to London for a round of balls, theatre visits and parties. They returned to their country estates for grouse-shooting, fox-hunting, balls and parties in the autumn. Their life has been described as 'eating, dancing, gossiping and flirting'. The scene of this Tissot painting is a rich London party in 1875. The performer (probably the host's daughter) is about to play the violin, but some couples are more interested in each other, hence the title: 'Hush!'

THINK ABOUT IT

1. Carefully study Sources E–J. Can you find examples in the sources of the 'two nations' described by Disraeli.

2. Which scene would have been most likely to appeal to Dickens as a subject to write about? Give a reason for your answer.

3. Choose one picture from Sources E–J that will form the basis of your description.

   ● Make an detailed list of everything you see in the picture(s), especially (where possible) the contrast of rich and poor.

   ● Using your list of items from the picture(s) think of some exciting adjectives and verbs to describe them.

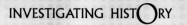

Pulling it Together

What was life like in Dickens' London?

Dickens loved London and hated London. In the novel *David Copperfield*, as the hero approaches London for the first time, Dickens makes him comment that it was 'an amazing place…full of wonders and wickedness'.

This assignment asks you to write your own 'Dickens' passage, describing a scene you saw on a tourist trip to London. The picture sources will allow you to describe what you did (for instance going on a bus, or visiting Newgate, or going to a ball) or an example of the 'underside' of life that you saw.

Stage 1 Preparation

1. Decide 'who' you are going to be, and why you are in London. Note that the storyline does not need to be exciting – something as simple as a trip to see a relative. Beware of making it so extreme as to become preposterous.

2. Re-read Sources B–D on pages 36–37, to remind yourself about Dickens' writing style.

3. Look again at the source you have chosen to be the basis of your description. Decide what effect you are going to give to your description. Think about the ways in which the people, place and weather will reflect the atmosphere for your reader.

Stage 2 The task

1. Write a recount of an imaginary visit to London you have made, in the form of an article in a nineteenth-century newspaper in the style of Charles Dickens, so it will contain factual details but also plenty of description.

2. Start with an opening sentence describing how you came upon the place, then describe it as authentically as you can.

3. Remember when you are writing:

- to choose your adjectives and adverbs carefully to achieve the effect you want

- Dickens uses complex sentences with a number of clauses and phrases

- to describe the poor people in a very sentimental way

- that your descriptions of the people, the place and the atmosphere must be sustained throughout your writing.

4. Write a first draft, then read it to a partner. Revisit the Dickens passages in Sources B–D and compare how successfully your passage copies his style of writing. Redraft your writing making any changes you have noted with your partner.

(a) The basic account *will tell a story of a trip to London, mentioning some places and people.*

(b) A better account *will include detailed, vivid descriptions of places and people.*

(c) The very good account *will describe the contrast between rich and poor in its descriptions of places and people.*

(d) The best account *will reflect the style of Dickens, using language to create a vibrant, authentic-sounding description.*

CHAPTER 4

Victorian Religion

Did God die in the nineteenth century?

In this chapter you will:

- **Consider how important religion was in people's lives.**
- **Consider whether Christianity declined in the nineteenth century.**
- **Conduct a 'SWOT' analysis for religion at the end of the nineteenth century.**

SOURCE A

This painting by Henry Alexander Bowler is called **The Doubt – Can these dry bones live?** *(1856). A young woman watches two butterflies, as she leans on a gravestone of a man called John Faithful. On the stone are inscribed the words: 'I am the Resurrection and the Life', and on the next gravestone the Latin word* Resurgam, *meaning 'I shall rise'.*

On 30 March 1851, the government conducted a **census** of religious belief. It found that $7\frac{1}{4}$ million people had gone to church that day (40% of the population) in 34,467 church buildings.

Although we would think these figures high today, at the time people were disappointed that so many people – particularly from the working classes – did not attend church.

Some historians have claimed that religion and the Church declined in Victorian Britain. This chapter will investigate whether that claim is true.

THINK ABOUT IT

1. **What symbols of death and life can you see in the painting?**

2. **What question is the painting asking, and what is its answer?**

3. **What does the painting suggest about Victorian beliefs about life after death?**

How important was religion in people's lives?

Religion filled people's lives. The parson was usually a J P and a Guardian of the Union Poor House. As **parson**, he received tithes (an annual 10% tax paid to the church) from all the people in his parish; as landowner, he received rents from his tenants. The church ran the schools. The calendar was organised around the Church's year – Lady Day (rents); St Valentine's Day; Easter and Christmas. And Church socials, musical evenings, choir, Sunday School outings and the like formed the backbone of social life.

SOURCE Ⓐ

This painting – **The Awakening Conscience** *by Holman Hunt (1854) – was the first painting to tackle the subject of prostitution. In the painting a woman – by Victorian standards, indecently dressed and (by sitting on the knee of a man who was not her husband) behaving badly – remembers her childhood faith and decides to change her life. A Bible text accompanied the painting – 'Behold your God' – and the picture is full of religious symbolism.*

Can you see:

- *The cat, toying with the bird (as the man is toying with her).*
- *The glove, carelessly dropped (as the man will cast her off when he is bored with her).*
- *The tapestry of vines being eaten by birds (symbolising her life being destroyed).*
- *The flowers (a warning that good looks will fade).*
- *The painting over the fire (showing the Bible story of the women taken in adultery).*
- *A bright shaft of light (showing her sudden change of mind).*

SOURCE B

The village church

If the people in Lark Rise had been asked their religion, the answer of nine out of ten of them would have been 'Church of England', for practically all of them were christened, married and buried as such. There were a few keener spirits. The family at the inn was Catholic. There were also three Methodist families which met in one of their cottages on Sunday evenings, but most of them attended church as well…

The church was fairly well filled, for it was a tiny place. The interior was almost as bare as a barn, with its grey, roughcast walls, plain-glass windows, and flagstone floor. The cold, damp, earthy odour common to old and unheated churches pervaded the atmosphere, with occasional whiffs of a more unpleasant nature said to proceed from the stacks of mouldering bones in the vault beneath…

The Squire's and clergyman's families had pews in the chancel, with backs to the wall on either side, and between them two long benches for the school-children. Below the steps down into the nave stood the harmonium, played by the clergyman's daughter, and round it was ranged a choir of small school-girls. Then came the rank and file of the congregation, nicely graded, with the farmer's family in the front row, then the Squire's gardener and coachman, the schoolmistress, the maidservants, and the cottagers, with the Parish Clerk at the back to keep order…

The service, with not a prayer left out or a creed spared, seemed to the children everlasting. They dared not so much as wriggle; they sat in their stiff, stuffy, best clothes, their stomachs lined with heavy Sunday dinner, in a kind of waking doze…

Many in the hamlet who attended neither church nor chapel guided their lives by the light of a few homely precepts such as 'Right's right and wrong's no man's right'. Strict honesty was the policy of most of them. For the afflicted or bereaved there was ready sympathy. In illness or trouble they were ready to help and to give to the small extent possible.

Flora Thompson, Lark Rise *(1939).*

◆ *In the book, Flora described her childhood in the 1880s at Juniper Hill ('Lark Rise'), a small village in Oxfordshire.*

THINK ABOUT IT

1. Make a list of all the things you can learn from pages 43–45 about Victorian religion. Divide them into religious, moral, economic and social issues.

2. Make a list of all the adjectives in the second paragraph of Source B. How do they affect the impression the author gives us about the church at Lark Rise?

3. Flora Thompson's vicar often preached on 'the absolute rightness of the social order as it then existed'. Explain using the third paragraph of Source B how the church was used to maintain the *status quo* (the 'way things were') and to keep things as they always had been.

4. 'Victorian religion was about what you did, not what you believed.' Do Sources A and B justify this comment on Victorian religion?

STOP AND REFLECT:
Write a paragraph explaining how important religion was in people's lives in the Victorian era.

How was religion attacked in the nineteenth century?

Christ in the house of his parents *by John Everett Millais (1850) showed an English-looking Jesus, having cut his hand, being kissed by his mother. Victorian Christians were scandalised because the carpenter's workshop had wood shavings on the floor, and the Holy Family were portrayed as being poor.*

In Victorian Britain, Christianity was attacked from three sides:

In 1835 Marian Evans (famous as the author George Eliot) translated *Das Leben Jesu* (*The Life of Jesus* – a book by the German theologian David Srauss) into English. Soon more books by German and French theologians became available. These writers tried to strip the 'Jesus of history' from the 'myths' of the Christian faith. They rejected the Bible, denied the Resurrection and ridiculed the miracles.

All this was very shocking to Victorian Christians. Translating *Das Leben Jesu* made George Eliot ill. Many famous people (such as the author Thomas Hardy and the psychiatrist Sigmund Freud) lost their faith in God. Ordinary people found their faith was shaken.

SOURCE A

Creation

Heaven and earth were created together, in the same instant. This work took place and Man was created on 23 October, 4004 BC, at nine o'clock in the morning.

Dr John Lightfoot, Vice-Chancellor of Cambridge University (1859).

SOURCE B

An Agnostic

I gradually came to disbelieve in Christianity…

We can no longer argue that, for instance, the beautiful hinge of a shell must have been made by an intelligent Being, like the hinge of a door by man. There seems to be no more design in living creatures than in the course which the wind blows. Everything in nature is the result of fixed laws…

The mystery of the beginning of all things is insoluble by us; and I for one must be content to remain an Agnostic.

Charles Darwin, Autobiography (1880).

Secondly, Communists, such as Engels (see page 19) and Karl Marx (who lived in London after 1851), also attacked Christianity. They saw religion as a trick to keep the poor in their place. Marx described religion as opium (a drug), which numbed the minds of poor people to their suffering: 'Religion is the sign of an oppressed creature, the heart of a heartless world. It is the opium of the people'.

SOURCE C

Monkey business
This cartoon mocks the idea of evolution by showing Darwin as a big monkey.

SOURCE D

If…

If evolution is true, religion is a lie, human law is a mass of foolishness and a base injustice; morality is moonshine; our labours for the black people of Africa were works of madness; and man and woman are only better beasts.

Adam Sedgewick, Professor of Geology at the University of Cambridge (1844).

THINK ABOUT IT

1. Make brief notes on the three developments that undermined religion in the nineteenth century under the headings Theology, Communism and Science.

2. 'Chat rooms and atom bombs! As a god, science has turned out to be either worthless or evil, and – a century and a half after Huxley – we still need religion to guide our lives.' Have a class discussion. Do you agree? Or should we 'put our faith in science'?

The third development that rocked Christianity was **evolution**. Based on a fundamental belief in the Bible, the Church taught that God had created the world in a single act (Source A). Charles Darwin, in *The Origin of Species* (1859) suggested that life had evolved.

The key question, of course, was 'How did we get here?' Before Darwin, religion had claimed to have the answer: *Creation*. Now science had provided an alternative – 'the survival of the fittest' – an automatic mechanism that did not need the idea of a God in control (Source B).

A number of scientists argued that, in this way, Science disproved Christianity, and in 1869 T H Huxley invented the word **agnostic**, meaning a person who believes it impossible ever to prove whether there is a 'God'. For Huxley, humankind needed to put its faith, not in God, but in science: 'Cherish her, venerate her, follow her methods carefully, and the future of this people will be greater than the past'.

It is quite possible to be a Christian **and** to believe in evolution. However, the Church decided to fight the new claims by persecuting the people who made them. Darwin was viciously criticised and mocked (Source C).

The Church opposed the new ideas by stressing how damaging they were (Source D). They hoped to turn people against the ideas, but all they did was to give ordinary people the idea that evolution disproved God.

STOP AND REFLECT: Theology, Communism and Science – write a sentence about each to suggest how each idea damaged the Christian faith.

What evidence is there of faith in the nineteenth century?

Renewal

After 1833, some people sought to renew the Church of England. The Anglo-Catholics (or 'High Churchmen', as they were called) wanted to go back to the ritual of the Middle Ages, and to decorate the churches with candles and flowers. They raised money to restore their churches. The Anglo-Catholics did well in the poor areas of the towns, where their colourful services were preferred to the dull Church of England service.

Revival

In 1859 a religious **revival** started in Northern Ireland. The effects were so great that courts closed because there were no criminals, pubs closed down and the local newspaper could not be published because all the journalists were praying.

Other revivals followed. In 1873–5, the American preacher D L Moody and the hymn-writer Ira D Sankey conducted a mission tour of the United Kingdom. Among the thousands saved were the Chairman and 17 members of the Edinburgh **Atheists**' Society.

Salvation

In the East End of London, a preacher named William Booth realised that religion was as much about people's bodies as their souls. 'What is the use of preaching the Gospel to men whose whole attention is concentrated upon a mad, desperate struggle to keep themselves alive?'

In 1878 Booth formed the **Salvation Army**. His down-and-outs did not know any hymns, so they sang simple choruses to popular song tunes. 'Why should the devil have all the best tunes,' he said.

Booth set up hostels, night shelters and cheap food depots. He founded a missing persons bureau, a job centre to help people find work, and a poor man's bank (which made small loans to skilled workers to buy tools).

SOURCE Ⓐ

A Revival – Wales in 1904

The meeting on Thursday night…commenced at seven o'clock and they lasted without break until 4:30 a.m. on Friday morning. During the whole time the congregation were under the influence of deep religious fervour and exaltation. There were about 400 people present in the Chapel when I took my seat at about nine o'clock ….

I had not been many minutes in the building before I felt that this was no ordinary gathering. Instead of the set order of proceedings to which we are accustomed at the normal religious service, everything here was left to the spontaneous impulse of the moment… A young woman rose to give out a hymn which was sung with deep earnestness. While it was being sung, several people dropped down from their seats as if they had been struck, and commenced crying for pardon…

At 2:30, a well-known resident then rose and said that salvation had come to him. The whole congregation then fell upon their knees, prayers ascending from every part of the building, while the preacher gave way to tears at the sight. This state of fervency lasted for about ten minutes…

Western Mail (12 & 15 November 1904).

◆ *In all, 100,000 people were converted in the Welsh revival.*

SOURCE **B**

A picture from In Darkest England and the Way Out, *by William Booth. What is symbolised, do you think, by: the raging sea?; the drowning people?; the people in uniform pulling the drowning people from the sea?; the lighthouse?; the Rock where the drowning people are saved?*

By 1900 the Salvation Army had served 27 million cheap meals, lodged 11 million homeless people, traced 18,000 missing people and found jobs for 9000 unemployed people.

Female workers known as '**slum** sisters' went to live in the poorest areas, setting an example of cleanliness and respectability, helping where possible, and talking about Jesus.

SOURCE **C**

There are all sorts of men; casuals, gaol birds, Out-of-Works, who have come there for the first time. And there are men who have at last seen a hope of escaping from that dreadful whirlpool into which their sins and misfortunes had drawn them, and of being restored to those comforts that they had feared so long were gone for ever; nay, of rising to live a true and Godly life. These tell their mates how this has come about, and urge all who hear them to try for themselves and see whether it is not a good and happy thing to be soundly saved.

William Booth, In Darkest England and the Way Out *(1890).*

THINK ABOUT IT

1. From Source A, list all the evidence of 'deep religious fervour and exaltation' at the meeting.

2. List all the strategies that William Booth used to get men and women interested in God. Suggest reasons why he was so successful.

STOP AND REFLECT: Find and list all the evidence on pages 48–49 to show that religion was still 'alive and well' in the late-nineteenth century.

What did missionaries do?

SOURCE A

God loved a lost world and gave His only Son to be a missionary. I love a lost world and I am a missionary, heart and soul. In this service I hope to live and in it I wish to die.

The more I become acquainted with barbarians, the more disgusting does heathenism become. Oh, Almighty God, help! help! and leave not this wretched people to the slave-dealer and Satan. Help them to look to Christ and live.

David Livingstone

SOURCE B

Either Christ is Lord of all, or He is not Lord at all.

James Hudson Taylor

SOURCE C

In China, it was thought a disgrace to bear a girl child. This print shows missionaries stopping disappointed parents burying a baby girl alive.

After 1850, many Christians wished 'that the light of the glorious gospel of truth may shine throughout the world' (Source A). Also, as westerners came into contact with native customs, there was a desire to 'rescue' the people from 'heathen ignorance' (Source C). Most missionaries believed in what came to be called the 'Three Cs' – Christianity, Commerce, Civilisation.

By 1900 there were 61,000 **missionaries** and more than 41 million Christians in Africa, Asia and the Pacific. In 1907 the British and Foreign Bible Society announced that, in the last century, it had printed and distributed 203,931,768 Bibles and **tracts**.

Sometimes missionaries showed respect for native peoples. For instance, the Mission to Delhi sought to adapt Christianity so that Hindus could accept it more easily.

One historian calls the missionary achievement 'spectacular' and claims that it 'showed what vitality the Christian religion could still inspire'.

THINK ABOUT IT

1. Suggest two reasons people went abroad as missionaries.

2. Were the westerners right to interfere in Source C? Did the Chinese not have the right to their own customs and way of life?

3. Do you think Source C is reliable?

4. From the sketches of missionaries' lives on page 51, find examples of missionaries:
   - doing medical work
   - setting up schools
   - accepting native culture
   - opposing cruel customs
   - benefiting the community
   - trusting God
   - wanting to spread the gospel.

MISSIONARIES FACT FILE

FACT FILE

After gaining medical experience **James Hudson Taylor** went as a missionary to China in 1858. He ignored laws forbidding westerners to go into the interior. When in 1870 his wife and two of their children died of cholera, Taylor wrote: 'I am cast down but not forsaken. Jesus is my life and strength.'

One day a man asked him why he had put his coat on back-to-front. Thereafter, Taylor wore Chinese dress, realising that his western clothes were getting in the way of the gospel message. He translated the New Testament into the Ningpo dialect. Taylor established 205 mission stations with 849 missionaries from England and 125,000 Chinese Christians.

FACT FILE

In 1876, at the age of 28, **Mary Slessor** went to Nigeria. Her main work there was saving twins – who were considered bad luck and were put to death by the local people.

She wrote: 'Raiding, plunder – the stealing of slaves – have almost entirely ceased. No chief ever died without the sacrifice of many lives, but this custom has now ceased. Drinking, especially among the women, is on the decrease. They are eager for education; and they are friendly to any one who will help them towards a higher plane of living.'

FACT FILE

In 1841 **David Livingstone** went to work as a missionary in South Africa. Soon he was going into unmapped areas, seeking sites for future missions. 'I place no value on anything I have or may possess,' he wrote. His explorations included walking 1500 miles across Africa from east to west, and the discovery of Victoria Falls in 1855. Livingstone helped to destroy the Arab slave trade, which he called 'the open sore of the world'.

FACT FILE

C T Studd was a brilliant cricketer, but in 1885 gave it up to go as a missionary to China. When his father died, leaving him a large fortune, Studd immediately gave most of it away, apart from £3400 which he set aside for his wife-to-be. When she found out she made him give away the rest. In 1910 he ignored doctor's advice and went as a missionary to Africa, where he died in 1931. His dying breath was: 'Hallelujah!'

FACT FILE

William Carey went as a missionary to India in 1794. In the next 25 years, Carey organised the translation of the Bible into 30 different Indian languages, set up mission schools and a College, founded the Agricultural Society of India, and campaigned for the abolition of sutee (the tradition that an Indian widow had to jump onto her husband's funeral pyre and be burned to death).

STOP AND REFLECT: From the information on pages 50–51, choose your five 'Most Amazing Facts about Missionaries'.

Pulling it Together

Did God die in the nineteenth century?

The issue of this chapter has been the fortunes of Christianity in late-Victorian Britain – both its problems, and its successes.

When an organisation is struggling, it often calls in management consultants, who carry out what is called a 'SWOT' analysis, that is, an analysis of the organisation's Strengths, Weaknesses, Opportunities and Threats. The strengths and weaknesses are an analysis of how the organisation is doing in the present; the opportunities and threats look forward to what it may have to face in the future.

Strengths	Weaknesses
• 41 million believers overseas	• German and French theologians
Opportunities	**Threats**

To do this assessment, you must imagine that you are a management consultant who has been called in by the Archbishop of Canterbury to do a SWOT analysis on the state of religion at the end of the nineteenth century.

Stage 1 Preparation

1. Work, preferably, in a group of four.

2. In your group, work through pages 43–51, finding all the Strengths and Weaknesses of religion at the end of the nineteenth century (to help, I have started you off with two ideas).

3. In your group, study pages 43–51 again, thinking of some hopes and fears for religion for the coming century (this will be harder).

4. Decide how you are going to present your report. Possible alternatives include a written report, a web-page, a presentation on PowerPoint or Overhead Projector, a poster, a talk, a cartoon strip, imaginary interviews etc. Consider your choice of medium carefully and make sure that it will suit the information being presented and also your audience.

Stage 2 Making the presentation

You must imagine that you are a management consultant doing a SWOT presentation on the state of religion at the end of the nineteenth century.

(a) The basic presentation *will give some facts about faith in the nineteenth century.*

(b) A better presentation *will list correctly some of the Strengths and Weaknesses of Christianity, and some Opportunities and Threats facing the Church, at the end of the nineteenth century.*

(c) A very good presentation *will give an extensive SWOT analysis, explaining how each issue is a Strength, a Weakness, an Opportunity or a Threat.*

(d) In the *best presentations, this will be done via a chosen medium which suits the information being presented, and will be lively, interesting and thought-provoking.*

CHAPTER 5

Ruling Britannia
Did the Victorians invent democracy?

In this chapter you will:

- Learn about the constitutional developments that created Britain's democracy.
- Criticise the British political system in the nineteenth century.
- Debate whether or not Britain was a democracy in 1914, and come to a personal conclusion.

Thomas Babington Macaulay (1800–59) became an MP, an official in India and, in 1839–41, Secretary of War.

Macaulay believed that England was the happiest country in the world. Looking at other countries (which were troubled with revolutions), he asked himself, why was Britain so peaceful and prosperous?

His answer was – 1688, when the Glorious Revolution saved Parliament from James II, and gave the British people freedom.

Most nineteenth-century writers agreed with Macaulay and, since most of them were members of the Whig Party, this view became known as 'The Whig Interpretation of History' – that the wonderful British Parliament was the basis of British freedom.

But were they correct?

This symbolic picture – 'The British Beehive' (1840) by the cartoonist George Cruickshank – shows Queen Victoria as the head of state. Beneath her are the House of Commons and the House of Lords, underpinned by Trial by Jury, freedom of religion, law and equality. Supporting everything are all the arts and industries of 'the richest country in the world'.

This chapter is arranged in two sections in the form of a debate. The first section argues that Britain did have a remarkable **democracy** in the nineteenth century. The second looks at the same facts, but argues that Britain was far from democratic, even in 1914.

THINK ABOUT IT

1. Discuss, 'What is democracy'? What is the minimum a country has to have in place before we might call it a 'democracy'?

2. From the Fact File, choose the three events that seem to you to be very important. Justify your choice to the class.

FACT FILE

A Parliamentary Timeline

1688 The Glorious Revolution – the British chase out James II, and establish rule by Parliament.

1715 George I of Hanover became king. There were two parties in Parliament, the Whigs (who supported the succession) and the Tories (who opposed it).
Septennial Act – Parliaments to sit for seven years.

1763 John Wilkes, a radical MP, accused the Prime Minister, Lord Bute, of lying.

1819 Peterloo massacre.

1832 The Great Reform Act (abolished 'rotten boroughs' and gave the vote to the £10 householders). The Whig Party is now called 'the Liberal Party'.

1838 The **Chartists**' *People's Charter* was published. Chartist petitions were presented in 1839, 1842 and 1848 – all were rejected.

1858 Abolition of **property qualification** for MPs.

1867 Second Reform Act (extended the vote to all male householders).

1872 Ballot Act (allowed voters to make a secret vote).

1884 Third Reform Act (extended the electorate to almost all British males over 21).

1885 Redistribution of Seats Act created **constituencies** of equal size.

1879–80 Gladstone's Midlothian election campaign.

1892 Kier Hardie elected as a 'Labour Party' candidate for West Ham.

1893 Independent Labour Party founded at Bradford.

1897 The National Union of Women's **Suffrage** Societies (the '**Suffragists**') was formed to campaign peacefully for the vote.

1900 Labour Representation Committee formed by the trade unions to finance Labour Party candidates.

1903 The Women's Social and Political Union (the '**Suffragettes**') was formed to fight for the vote for women.

1906 General Election: 29 Labour Party candidates elected to the House of Commons.

1911 Parliament Act (the House of House could not veto an Act passed by the House of Commons. Parliaments to sit for five years. MPs to be paid.)

1918 Women over 30 allowed to vote.

1924 First Labour government, with Ramsay MacDonald as Prime Minister.

1928 Women over 21 allowed to vote.

Argument One: YES!

The Prime Minister

In 1715 George I of Hanover became king. This put a Protestant on the throne and secured the survival of Parliament.

But there was another advantage. George I was German and could not speak English. Instead of running the country himself, he left it to the most powerful man in Parliament – a minister called Robert Walpole, who became his *Prime* (meaning 'First') *Minister*.

This system, in which the monarch appoints a government headed by the leader of the largest party in Parliament, is the system we still have today.

Wilkes and liberty

John Wilkes was an MP who wanted Parliamentary reform. In 1763 he accused the Prime Minister, Lord Bute, of lying. He was imprisoned, then outlawed. People were outraged. Wilkes was elected MP for Middlesex. When the government cancelled his election result, the people simply elected him again! Thousands of people all over the country protested. In the end he won and was allowed to become an MP.

Wilkes established the principle of freedom of speech, the idea that in Britain it is OK to criticise the government.

The House of Commons in 1808. It is arranged so that MPs can debate laws. It is open government – members of the public watch from the Public Gallery (newspaper reporters were given places in there after 1803). Foreign writers said that the British Parliamentary system was the best system of government in the world.

Wilberforce and the abolition of the slave trade

Every year from 1788 to 1807, William Wilberforce presented a bill to Parliament, trying to get the slave trade abolished. His supporters published leaflets and books, and went round the country giving speeches. In the end, Wilberforce won: the MPs were persuaded, and the slave trade was abolished in 1807.

Wilberforce's campaign was the first ever in modern history that mobilised public opinion to get a change in the laws. Wilberforce's campaign formed a model for future British political life.

> ### THINK ABOUT IT
>
> 1. Using page 55 only, make a list of facts about 'the British Constitution 1715–1815' (e.g. there was a king).
>
> 2. Which of these 'aspects of the British constitution' still survive today?

SOURCE A

A poster, drawn by a Whig artist, celebrating the Reform Act. At the top are King William IV, and Lord Grey and the other Whig leaders. The roaring lion represents the British people. At the bottom left the opponents of reform flee. At the bottom right, Britannia (personifying Britain) looks on with drawn sword.

The Great Reform Act, 1832

By 1830, Parliament had been in existence for more than 500 years, and during that time Britain had changed. Some places that had been busy towns were now only tiny villages. Yet these 'rotten boroughs', as they were called, still sent two MPs to Parliament. At the same time, huge industrial towns that had grown up during the Industrial Revolution, such as Manchester and Birmingham, had no MPs.

The Whig government of Lord Grey wished to reform Parliament, but at first the bill was thrown out by the House of Lords. In 1832 the King forced the House of Lords to pass the bill by threatening to create 50 new lords.

It is impossible to overestimate the importance of The Great Reform Act of 1832. It abolished 56 rotten boroughs and created 63 new seats in Parliament for towns in the north. Also, the vote was given to all men owning property worth more than £10 a year, increasing the number of voters by 50%. But it also established two key principles which opened the door to future reforms:

- that the people have a right to be represented in Parliament

- that the House of Lords **must** give way to the House of Commons, which represents the will of the People.

SOURCE B

The Reform Act of 1832 showed the growing freedom of the English political mind. It gave the vote to the middle class, set free the House of Commons from **aristocratic** control, and led by a natural sequence to democracy and other reforms. It was the peaceful acceptance by the country of the democratic claims of an industrial age.

H A L Fisher, History of Europe *(1935).*

THINK ABOUT IT

1. Discuss Source A. What can you see? Who drew it, and why? Explain the message of the poster.

2. Some historians think Britain became a democracy in 1832. Find five facts that might support such a claim.

3. Write a persuasive essay with five paragraphs: 'Why the Reform Act was Important for British Democracy'.

   - Write in the form of topic sentence ('point') plus supporting explanation.

   - Finish with a conclusion, starting: 'Therefore it is clear that the Reform Act was very important…'

Benefits to the people

In the 1840s, laws were passed to improve the conditions of ordinary people (for example, Factory Acts, a Mines Act and a Public Health Act). In 1846 the Corn Laws (which had kept the price of bread high) were abolished. The philosophy behind these measures was called '**utilitarianism**' ('the greatest happiness for the greatest number') which, when you think about it, is a very democratic ideal.

More reforms

In 1867, the Second Reform Act extended the vote again – to all men who had a house – and almost doubled the electorate.

Perhaps the most important change of all occurred in 1872, when the Ballot Act abolished voting in public, and allowed voters to make a secret vote, by placing their ballot paper in a **ballot** box. This stopped bribery and bullying in elections. In 1884, the Third Reform Act further extended the electorate, so that every British male who was not a criminal, a lord or a lunatic could vote.

Government for the people

Government **by** the People led to laws **for** the people. In the 1870s a national system of education was set up and trade unions were made legal. Old age pensions were introduced in 1908.

Finally, in 1909–10, David Lloyd George, the **Chancellor of the Exchequer**, increased taxes to pay for a system of National Insurance, to protect workers from ill-health and unemployment. This was called 'the People's **Budget**'.

SOURCE C

At first, the House of Lords rejected the People's Budget. This led the Liberal government of the time to introduce the Parliament Act (1911) which stated that the House of House could not veto, only delay (for two years), an Act passed by the House of Commons.

THINK ABOUT IT

1. Explain why the Ballot Act might have 'stopped bribery and bullying in elections'.

2. Study Source C.

   Find four devices the artist uses to influence the viewer to support the government against the House of Lords.

The Midlothian Campaign

The Reform Act and the Ballot Act changed the way politicians campaigned for votes. In 1879–80, in Midlothian in Scotland, Prime Minister William Gladstone held a series of mass rallies, copying the revival meetings of Sankey and Moody (see page 48). Each meeting began with Liberal songs, set to hymn tunes, followed by stirring speeches. Newspapermen were invited, so they could spread the message to the whole country.

The rise of the Labour Party

After the workers had been given the vote, it was only a matter of time before there was a political party for the workers. Its leader was a Scottish trade unionist called Kier Hardie, who in 1892 had been elected as 'Labour Party' candidate for West Ham.

On 13 January 1893, 120 delegates met at Bradford to found the Independent Labour Party. In 1900, the trade unions formed a Labour Representation Committee to support and finance Labour candidates and, on 12 February 1906, 29 Labour MPs took their seats in the House of Commons, calling themselves 'the Labour Party'.

The Labour Party grew quickly (the introduction of payment of MPs in 1911 helped poor men enter Parliament) and in 1924 it formed a government, with Ramsay MacDonald as the first Labour Prime Minister.

SOURCE D

The Enthusiasm of Early Labour

Many young men who were Methodist local preachers were attracted to the movement by the principles of Socialism. It was politics inspired by religious fervour. 'Vocal Unions' were formed which went with cyclist corps into the country at weekends, and audiences were gathered on village greens by the singing of the choirs; then short, simple talks on Socialism were given. On their country jaunts the cyclists distributed leaflets and pasted slips on gates, and sometimes stuck them on cows, with such slogans as 'Workers of the World Unite!'

Philip Snowden, Autobiography *(1934).*

◆ *Snowden travelled the country giving talks recruiting people to the Labour Party. A friend joked that his talks always ended with 'a bit of "Come to Jesus" '.*

THINK ABOUT IT

Study Source D.

1. **Why did the Labour campaigners stick posters on cows?**

2. **What is meant by 'his talks always ended with a bit of "come to Jesus" '?**

3. **Find two other ways the early Labour Party was influenced by religion.**

4. **Suggest reasons why the campaigns had such a 'religious' feel to them.**

STOP AND REFLECT: From pages 55–58, make a list of all the good and positive facts and developments you can find about the British political system in the nineteenth century.

Argument Two: NO!

Britain's political system in the eighteenth century was not a democracy – it was totally corrupt, as Hogarth's painting (Source E) showed!

Before 1832, there were very few voters (only about 450,000 in the whole country, out of a population of $6\frac{1}{2}$ million). This meant that rich people could afford to *buy* their way into Parliament. Some 'rotten boroughs' had very few voters, some places no voters at all – these places were called 'pocket boroughs' because they were in the gift of the local landowner. The most frightening truth about Hogarth's painting was that it was based upon a real election, in Oxfordshire in 1754, when the Duke of Marlborough bribed his way to success.

In the same way, MPs *sold* their support to the government in return for easy jobs as civil servants, or simply for money – as MPs went to vote, the government's agent would shake their hand, slipping gold coins into their hand (which is where we get the phrase 'a golden handshake').

SOURCE E

This painting by Hogarth shows electors – who have been bribed and brought in the candidate's private coach – voting. Voters had to swear on the Bible and an old soldier with only a hook for a hand is trying to take the oath, while a lawyer for the other side argues that he cannot do so, because he cannot put his right hand on the book. A criminal (his legs in shackles) whispers the right name into the ear of a simpleton who does not know what he is doing. Behind him two thugs (one of them having lost his nose to a sexually transmitted disease) drag a dying man to the voting booth.

Bad government

For a century the government consisted of a tiny, inter-married aristocracy. It did nothing to protect the workers or improve their condition – the 1790s were years of famine, when some people starved to death. When the French Revolution broke out in 1789, the government became very reactionary. In 1799 it passed laws to ban trade unions. In 1817, it even suspended **habeas corpus** (the law that prevents people being imprisoned without trial). Government spies (called **agents provocateurs**) encouraged people to plot rebellions, then arrested them.

Peterloo

On 16 August 1819, a rally of 50,000 people at St Peter's Field in Manchester called for the reform of Parliament.

It was peaceful, legal, and many men turned up with their wives and children. The local magistrates set the local militia on them.

There was a national outcry, but the government's reaction was merely to pass acts forbidding meetings, increasing the power of the police and preventing publications critical of the government.

*In 1819 at Peterloo – as the massacre came to be called – at least 15 died, and perhaps 500 were wounded. The magistrates arrested 35 people, including John Tyas, **The Times** reporter, who had simply been there to write about the events.*

SOURCE F

Reform Parliament!

It is the labour of those who toil which makes a country rich… With the correct idea of your own worth in your minds, with what indignation must you hear yourselves called the Rabble, the Mob, the Swinish Multitude…

The remedy consists wholly and solely of a reform of the Commons, or People's House of Parliament.

William Cobbett, Political Register (1816).

◆ *Calls for reform grew as time went on. The reformers wanted the vote for all men and women, an end to corruption and police spies, and the freedom of the press.*

THINK ABOUT IT

1. Re-write Source F in a modern style. Use a thesaurus to find alternative words.

2. Imagine it is 1831. Using pages 59–60, list any changes you would make.

3. Use your ideas to write a speech entitled 'The British political system must be reformed.' Remember that this will be a persuasive text:

   ● Start with an opening statement.

   ● Use repetition of particular phrases to emphasise your points clearly to your audience.

   ● Choose emotive words and phrases to influence your audience.

   ● Give particular examples to illustrate your points.

   ● Finish with a memorable concluding sentence.

The Chartists

When reform eventually arrived in 1832, it was far from democratic. George Eliot described the Reform Act of 1832 as 'a trick to keep the aristocracy in its place'. The number of voters remained tiny, and until 1850 three-quarters of the MPs in the House of Commons were from the upper classes.

In 1838 campaigners published a 'People's Charter', demanding a place for working men in the political system. Its supporters – the 'Chartists', as they came to be called – collected a petition with 1,200,000 signatures, but when it was presented to Parliament in 1839, it was rejected.

FACT FILE

The Growing Electorate

Date	No. Voters	No. Adults	%age
1830	450,000	6½ million	7
1832	650,000	6½ million	10
1867	2,000,000	10 million	20
1884	5,000,000	11 million	45

SOURCE G

The Chartists' Demands

1. The vote for all men over 21.

2. Annual Parliaments.

3. Vote by secret ballot.

4. Constituencies of equal size.

5. Abolition of the property qualification for MPs.

6. Payment of MPs.

From the 1838 Charter.

◆ *Using the Fact File on page 54, find out how many of the Chartists' demands were eventually achieved.*

A Chartist uprising in Newport in November 1839 was easily put down.

In 1842, the Chartists presented a second petition, with 3,300,000 signatures but, despite strikes and a spate of terrorism called the 'Plug Plots', Parliament rejected it again. Another vast petition was presented, and rejected, in 1848.

In fact, few people in Britain in the nineteenth century wanted democracy. Macaulay believed that democracy would destroy the nation, and wrote: 'it is by property and intelligence that the nation ought to be governed'. Even in 1906, *true* democracy – 'government by the people, for the people' – seemed still a long way away (see Source H).

SOURCE H

Manifesto

To the Electors:

• This election is to decide whether or not Labour is to be represented in Parliament.

• The House of Commons is supposed to be the people's House, and yet the people are not there.

• The aged poor are neglected. The slums remain. Underfed school-children are still neglected.

• You have it in your power to see that Parliament carries out your wishes.

Vote Labour.

Labour Party manifesto for the 1906 General Election (see page 58).

THINK ABOUT IT

1. **Looking at the six Chartist demands (Source G), which do you think was the most important for democracy?**

2. **In what ways is Source H like Source F?**

SOURCE ❶

This W K Haselden cartoon – entitled 'The Revolt of the Dove' – was published in the **Daily Mirror** *on 15 April 1907.*

What is the message of the cartoon?

Votes for women

Until 1884 a Victorian wife was officially listed as one of her husband's possessions. Her expected role was to be her husband's helper and delight. By 1900 women had still not been given the right to vote in Parliamentary elections.

In 1897, the National Union of Women's Suffrage Societies (NUWSS) was formed. The 'Suffragists' as they were called, campaigned peacefully for the vote. They got nowhere.

Not only did many men oppose women's suffrage, many women opposed it too.

In 1903, therefore, Emmeline Pankhurst formed the Women's Social and Political Union (WSPU). The 'Suffragettes', as they came to be called, were much more militant (see Fact File).

If anything, however, the Suffragettes turned people against Women's Suffrage. Women did not get the vote until after the First World War.

SOURCE J

Why women should not have the vote

I maintain that the two sexes sitting together would no doubt alter the whole tone and whole feeling of this Parliament. I do not think that any man will deny that he is conscious – when he is debating with women – of a feeling of reserve, which is very different from the feeling which men have when they are discussing freely and debating freely with one another...

The way in which certain types of women have acted in the last year or two, lends a great deal of colour to the argument that the mental equilibrium of the female sex is not as stable as the mental equilibrium of the male sex... It seems to me that this House should remember that, if the vote is given to women, those who will take the greatest part in politics will not be the quiet, retiring, constitutional women...but those very militant women who have brought so much disgrace and discredit upon their sex. It would introduce a disastrous element into our public life... One feels that it is not cricket for women to use force... It is little short of nauseating and disgusting to the whole sex...

Where are the women merchants and the women bankers? Where are the women directors of great undertakings? Nowhere to be seen at the head of the great businesses of the country... It appears to me that it is one of the fundamental truths on which all civilisations have been built up, that it is men who have made and controlled the State, and I cannot help thinking that any country which departs from that principle must be undertaking an experiment which in the end will prove to be exceedingly dangerous...

I believe that the normal man and the normal woman both have the instinct that man should be the governing one of the two, and I think that the undoubted dislike that women have for men who are effeminate and which men have for masculine women is nothing more or less than the expression of this instinct...

Viscount Helmsley, speaking in Parliament, 28 March 1912.

◆ *The bill would have given the vote to about one million women voters. Women over 30 did not get the vote until 1918, and women over 21 not until 1928.*

FACT FILE

Tactics of the Suffragettes:

- They broke shop windows.
- They chained themselves to railings.
- They held mass meetings.
- They sent deputations to 10 Downing Street.
- They interrupted debates in the House of Commons from the Ladies Gallery.
- They burned down churches.
- They bombed Lloyd George's house.
- They assaulted policemen who tried to arrest them.
- When arrested, they went on Hunger Strike.
- In 1913, Emily Davison threw herself under the king's horse and was killed.

THINK ABOUT IT

1. Read Source J. Identify and explain the four reasons Helmsley gives why women should not have the vote.

2. From page 62, find two more reasons why men did not think women ought to have the vote.

STOP AND REFLECT: From pages 59–63, make a list of all the bad and negative facts and developments you can find about the British political system in the nineteenth century.

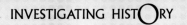

Pulling it Together

Did the Victorians invent democracy?

The issue of this chapter has been how democratic the British **constitution** of the nineteenth century was.

Whereas some historians are prepared to accept that Britain was a democracy from 1832, it is arguable that Britain was not a democracy until 1928, or even later. The British-based Centre for Citizenship comments: 'The British like to refer to the British Parliament as the "mother" of parliaments. They mean to imply that the democracy is their country's gift to the world. *But that is far from being the truth.*'

Yet, writing in 1902, a Russian, Moisei Ostrogorski, stated that 'hardly two generations back, Britain was still an aristocratic society; at the present moment she is completely drawn into the democratic process'.

Your task is to write a report agreeing or disagreeing with him.

Stage 1 Preparation

1. Have a class debate: 'Was Britain a democracy in 1914?' Pupils who studied pages 55–58 can argue for the motion; those who studied pages 59–63 can argue against it. Be careful to debate properly: stay relevant, and address the point made by the last speaker before making your own.

2. Working on your own, remembering the debate, make a list of points for, and a list of points that were made against the motion. Decide what your considered opinion is.

Stage 2 Writing the essay

Your essay title is 'Was Britain a democracy in 1914?' This will be a discursive text.

- First, write about all the reasons that Britain might be regarded as a democracy in 1914. Take a paragraph for each point.

- Next write about all the ways in which Britain was not truly democratic. Take a paragraph for each point.

- As you make each point, remember to explain it.

- Then finish your essay with a paragraph explaining your considered opinion about the original question.

(a) The basic essay presentation will give some facts about government in the nineteenth century.

(b) A better essay presentation will list correctly some of the good things about the British system of government, and some of the things that were less than democratic, in the nineteenth century.

(c) A very good essay presentation will explain some good things about the government, and why some things were still less than democratic by 1914.

(d) The best essay presentation will finish with a considered evaluation of the question, backing up the idea with facts.

CHAPTER 6

Heroes in the Hunt for Health

Who did the most for medicine in the nineteenth century?

SOURCE A

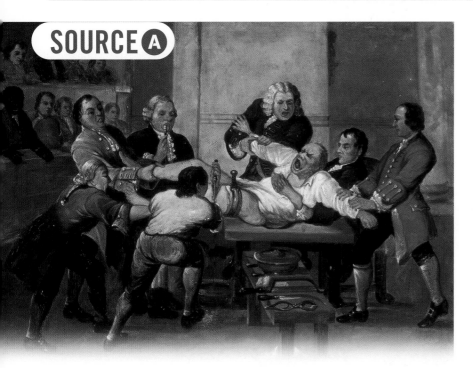

An operation to amputate a leg, c.1800. Today, a doctor doing an operation like this would be put in prison.

SOURCE B

Liston's Most Famous Operation

Amputated the leg under two-and-a-half minutes (the patient died afterwards from gangrene). He amputated in addition the fingers of his young assistant (who died afterwards from gangrene). He also slashed through the coat tails of a spectator, who was so terrified that the knife had cut him he dropped dead from fright. That was the only operation in history with a 300% mortality rate.

Richard Gordon, **Great Medical Disasters** *(1983).*

◆ *In the days before* **anaesthetics***, speed was essential in surgery and Robert Liston (1794–1847) was the fastest. In 1847, he cut his own finger during an operation, and died of gangrene.*

In this chapter you will:

- Consider the inadequacies of medical care in 1800.
- Study the medical advances made by six individuals.
- Develop a webpage to celebrate the individual who made the greatest contribution to promoting health.

Until 1800, medicine was barbaric. Just to *think* about operations like those in Source A makes you feel squeamish!

This chapter studies those wonderful people whose discoveries took medicine out of the dark ages. Forget Princess Diana, Brunel, Churchill and the like – it is the people you will learn about in *this* chapter who should be your *real* heroes!

THINK ABOUT IT

Make a list of things in Source A we would not allow to happen at an operation nowadays.

What were doctors like in 1800?

Medical care in 1800

Surgeons were able to operate with great speed, but their patients often died afterwards, usually of infection (see Source B), but also of bleeding or post-operative shock.

Doctors, meanwhile, ignorant of germs, were powerless against infectious disease until the discovery of **antibiotics** in the twentieth century. Their 'cures' (for instance, bleeding with leeches) often stopped the patient getting better naturally. A woman had a better chance of recovering after giving birth in the filthiest slum than in the best hospital in London.

SOURCE D

A Source of Infection

I remember the surgeon in the theatre with his threaded needles dangling from the front of an outworn old coat, stained with blood and spotted with pus… An old sister who had spent her life in the hospital once sadly said to me: 'I really do not think the doctors do much good, and as for the surgeons, I think they do as much harm as they do good'.

Memories of a doctor of hospitals in 1871.

THINK ABOUT IT

1. What does Source C suggest about doctors in the nineteenth century?

2. Compare the doctors in Sources C and E. Which doctor has more chance of curing his patient?

SOURCE C

*In this 1869 **Punch** cartoon, a doctor is visiting a fashionable patient. She is saying: 'Cod-liver oil!!! I couldn't take such horrible stuff as that' and he replies, 'Well, what would you say to a cream and orange liqueur?'*

SOURCE E

THINK ABOUT IT

1. Make a list of everything you can see in Source E. What was the message of the painting? How do you think the personal circumstances of the painter might have affected the message?

2. Imagine you are the mother in Source E. Write a letter to your sister telling her about your child's illness and about what the doctor did.

   In this personal letter, you will need to:

   - use first person, active, past tense
   - use connectives related to time (e.g. *'then'*) or contrast (e.g. *'however'*, *'yet'*)
   - use powerful adjectives, verbs and adverbs for this moving scene
   - vary the length of your sentences to create impact.

   Is the child going to live or die in your story?

Sir Luke Fildes' painting **The Doctor** *(1890). On the table are a bottle of medicine and a cup, but the doctor is looking at the child. The parents are in the shadows; the husband rests a hand on the mother's shoulder. At the cottage window dawn is just breaking. Fildes said that 'dawn is the critical time of all deadly illnesses'. Fildes' eldest son, Phillip, had died on Christmas morning, 1877, and the doctor had impressed Fildes greatly with his care and attention to his dying child.*

STOP AND REFLECT:
Write a paragraph explaining what you consider to be the **main** problem holding back medical care in 1800.

Who were the heroes of health?

Medical care advanced during the nineteenth century. This enquiry studies the people who made those advances, and asks you (page 71) to judge how important they were.

1. Before 1800, doctors had no way of stopping pain during an operation. One young doctor, **James Simpson,** so hated attending operations that he thought of giving up medicine and becoming a lawyer. Instead, he set about finding an effective anaesthetic. In 1847, he discovered chloroform. The popularity and general use of the new anaesthetic was assured when Queen Victoria took it to reduce the pain while giving birth in 1853.

Surgery ceased to be horrific. Surgeons could work more slowly and carefully, and the patient was left remembering nothing about the operation. In 1856 Simpson was awarded a prize by the French Academy of Sciences for the 'most important benefits done for humanity'.

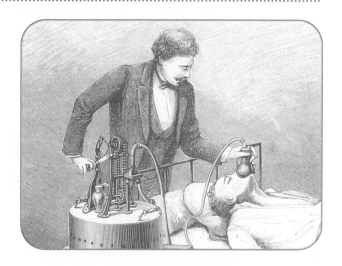

2. **Florence Nightingale** always wanted to be a nurse – even though for many years her father forbade her! In those days nursing was not a job for any but the least-educated, poorest girls.

In 1854, she took a team of nurses to the British Army hospital in the Crimea (Russia). Her standards of cleanliness and care were so high that she reduced the death rate there from 42% to 2%!

Her work in the Crimea made her famous as 'the lady with the lamp'. When she returned – although bed-ridden for the rest of her life – she almost single-handedly founded the modern profession of nursing, writing *Notes on Nursing* (1856) and setting up the Nightingale School for Nurses (1859).

SOURCE **F**

Thank God for Chloroform

Mr Dear Simpson,

Before the days of anaesthetics, a patient preparing for an operation was like a condemned criminal preparing for execution… The dread of pain keeps many a patient from submitting to operations which would save life…

When I first heard that anaesthetics had been discovered I could not believe it. I have since thanked God that He has put it into your heart to devise so simple and safe a way of lessening pain.

Yours most truly

An old patient

Florence Nightingale – the only one of our 'heroes' to get her picture on our money!

3. **Edwin Chadwick** was an expert on the Poor Law who noticed how much poverty was caused by ill-health. In 1848 an epidemic of **cholera** forced the government to listen to him, and in the same year a Public Health Act set up a Board of Health, run by Chadwick, with powers to appoint medical officers, build sewers, clean streets and inspect lodging houses.

Chadwick was an aggressive, overbearing person and – as soon as the crisis was over – MPs abolished the Board of Health and forced Chadwick to retire.

FACT FILE

Historians have said that Chadwick:
- invented public health
- made the breakthrough in public opinion that Public Health was necessary
- established that the *government* had to do something about health
- was the first person to use statistics to analyse public health
- realised that small circular sewage pipes were more efficient than larger ones
- realised you cannot dump sewage into rivers.

A 1983 BBC TV programme claimed he saved more lives than all the doctors put together.

---

4. **Louis Pasteur** was a brilliant scientist. In those days, scientists knew about bacteria, but Pasteur was the first to realise (1864) that it was bacteria that caused decay, e.g. that caused food to go bad.

In 1866, Pasteur's daughter died of **typhoid**. Motivated by her death, Pasteur began to work on another idea, that disease, too, was caused by bacteria. This idea was known as the germ theory of disease, and it changed the history of medicine. Realising that germs caused disease led directly to Joseph Lister's work on **antiseptics** (see page 70).

Then, in 1880, while studying the disease chicken cholera, one of Pasteur's researchers, by accident, injected some chickens with an old culture of the disease. The chickens became ill, but did not die. What was more, when the mistake was discovered and the chickens re-injected, they did not even get ill – Pasteur had discovered **inoculation**. Today, when you are inoculated against Measles or Rubella, or have your BCG injection, you are a testimony to Pasteur's work to prevent other people dying as his daughter had done.

FACT FILE

What historians have said about Pasteur:
- 'If one were to choose among the greatest benefactors of humanity, Louis Pasteur would certainly rank at the top. He set the stage for modern biochemistry.'
- 'The "germ theory of disease" is one of the most important in medical history. His work became the foundation for the science of microbiology, and a cornerstone of modern medicine.'
- 'The greatest biologist of the nineteenth century.'

Pasteur at work in his laboratory.

5. **Joseph Lister**, Professor of Surgery at Glasgow University, was researching sepsis (infection) in wounds. Although at that time operations were painless, half of his patients still died after an operation.

Lister suspected that this was caused by dirt, but even though he kept the wards clean, there was no improvement in the death rate.

In 1865, Lister read about Pasteur's germ theory of disease. He found that carbolic – a mild acid used to disinfect drains – killed germs. He cleaned wounds and bandages with it, and filled the air during operation with a carbolic spray.

Lister's post-operative mortality rate as a result of sepsis fell to 0%.

Lister was mocked and his ideas were unpopular, but surgeons were forced to change. By 1890, they had adopted sterile procedures: washing their hands, using rubber gloves and sterilising instruments.

Lister's discovery marked a turning point in surgery. Today historians split the history of surgery into 'Before Lister' and 'After Lister'.

Surgeons now dared to do more internal surgery. The first operation to remove an appendix was performed in 1888 (by Sir Frederick Treves – see page 9). In 1896, the first heart operation was carried out.

In 1892, at a meeting to honour Louis Pasteur, Pasteur turned and bowed to Lister, calling him 'the man who has done most for suffering humanity'.

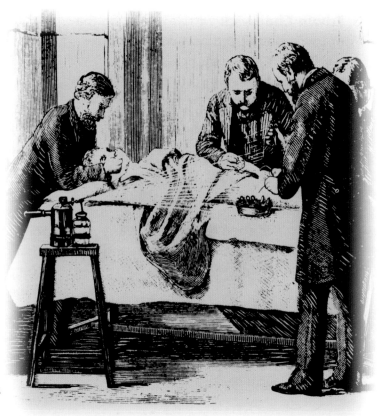

An operation c.1870. Note the anaesthetist holding a chloroform pad over the patient's nose. Even though the doctors wear ordinary clothes and do not 'scrub up', the antiseptic spray kills the germs.

SOURCE Ⓖ

Thank God for Lister

One of the most feared accidents a hundred years ago was the compound fracture, where the sharp end of the broken bone pierced the skin. Because it so often resulted in death from infection, most doctors would immediately amputate the victim's arm or leg. When I think about how many of our teenagers have come back with compound fractures from skiing or snowboarding, I give thanks for Joseph Lister.

Rev E. Hird, **Joseph Lister: Medical Revolutionary.**

6. In a study of York (1897–98), Benjamin Seebohm Rowntree found that 28% of the population fell below the minimum income, and 16% lived in absolute poverty.

The Chancellor of the Exchequer, **David Lloyd George**, was outraged by this. He introduced:

- 1908: Old Age Pensions.

- 1909: Labour Exchanges, to help the unemployed find jobs.

- 1911: National Insurance, for a contribution of 4d (about 2p) a week, a worker got free medical treatment when ill, and a little **dole** money if he was sick or unemployed.

These measures not only helped the poor but, because they established the principle that the state has an obligation to raise taxes to support to the poor, they heralded the introduction of the Welfare State after 1945.

A Liberal Party poster (1911)
- *The text reads: 'Mr Lloyd George's National Health Insurance Bill provides for the insurance of the Worker in case of Sickness'.*

THINK ABOUT IT

Choose your 'greatest hero of health'! Before you do so, consider:

1. Make a list of all the reasons the writer of Source F (page 68) valued the discovery of chloroform.

2. Is it relevant to the debate that Florence Nightingale has her face on a £10 note (page 68)?

3. Does it undermine Chadwick's claim to fame that he was sacked (page 69)?

4. Is it fair to credit Pasteur with the discovery of inoculation (page 69)?

5. 'Because of Lister, teenage boys can go snowboarding.' Is this the main message of Source G (page 70)?

6. How can Lloyd George be a candidate to be a 'hero of health' when nothing that he did was anything to do with medicine?

STOP AND REFLECT: For each of the six heroes in the hunt for health on pages 68–71:
- Make a list of what they **did**.
- Write an explanation showing why what they did was important.

Pulling it Together

Who did most for medicine in the nineteenth century?

The issue of this chapter has been to assess the importance of those individuals who in the period helped to make the people of Britain healthier.

While it is easy to think about what they did, and why they were important, it is a difficult thing to decide who was the most important, because they all made contributions in very different fields – public health, anaesthetics, pathology (the theory of what causes disease), antiseptics and welfare.

Stage 1 Preparation

1. Have a balloon debate: 'Who did most for health before 1910?' All the pupils choose a favourite 'hero for health' – Nightingale, Simpson, Chadwick, Pasteur, Lister or Lloyd George. They study their hero's life and contribution carefully, and prepare to argue their case.

Six pupils volunteer to be each of the 'heroes'. The idea is that they are all in a balloon that needs to lose weight to stay in the air. Only one can stay in the balloon – the one who convinces the rest of the class that they were the greatest hero in the hunt for health. The speakers put their case in turn. When they have finished the class takes a vote to decide, but you need to decide who you think *ought* to have won the debate.

2. When the class has finished this, working on your own, make a list of points for, and a list of points against the person you think ought to have won.

Stage 2 Writing the webpage

3. Imagine you have been asked to construct a webpage for the History department's 'Heroes of Health' website. Your brief is to produce a page on the person who gave the greatest services to health.

The page **must** explain what the person did, why they were important, and why they were more important than other contenders.

4. Decide how you are going to design your webpage to have maximum impact.

(a) The basic presentation *will give some facts about the chosen person.*

(b) A better presentation *will list correctly some of the achievements of the chosen person, explaining that these things were important.*

(c) A very good presentation *will list correctly some of the achievements of the chosen person, explaining why s/he was vital to the development of health.*

(d) The best presentation *will assess the comparative importance of their chosen person, proving that his/her contribution was more important than the work of others.*

CHAPTER 7

The Empire

Should Britons be proud of the British Empire?

In this chapter you will:

- Learn about the growth of the British Empire.
- Study British attitudes to the peoples of the Empire.
- Debate whether Britain ought to pay compensation for the slave trade.
- Conduct research studies on the Irish Famine and India.
- Write a persuasion text on whether pupils should study the British Empire.

Until 1958, 24 May was celebrated every year in Britain as 'Empire Day'. The British were immensely proud of their Empire. Maps in school classrooms showed the world coloured red. Children growing up in the age of Empire were thrilled by the wonder of it all – all those far-off places, peoples and products! In children's encyclopaedias they read, and unquestioningly accepted, that 'parts [of the world] must be ruled by white men for the good of the natives, who without proper control and leadership would remain in their original conditional of savagery'.

The British Empire in 1905.

It never occurred to them that the Empire might be racist, or even unpopular.

In the years after 1945, most countries in the Empire gained their **independence**. Historians in the newly independent nations wrote about the Empire as a shameful intrusion, a time of oppression and extortion which destroyed their culture and development.

Should we be proud, or ashamed, of the British Empire?

THINK ABOUT IT

Is the idea of Empire – one nation ruling over another – always wrong, or can a well-governed empire be alright?

How was the British Empire built?

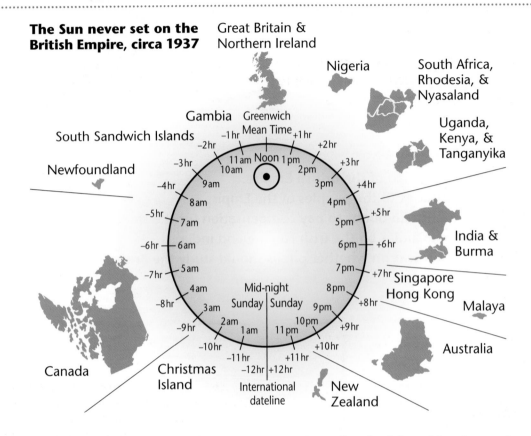

The Sun never set on the British Empire, circa 1937

In 1896 the British Empire spanned 11,335,000 square miles with 394,600,000 inhabitants. One list of places that were at some time part of the British Empire notes 284 places, from huge territories such as the sub-continents of India and Australia, to tiny islands with exotic names like Tristan da Cuhna. It was the Empire 'on which the sun never set'.

There was never a formal 'British Empire'. Only India was officially Britain's 'Empire'. Australia, South Africa, Canada and New Zealand were self-governing 'dominions'. Other areas were ruled in different ways. This was because the Empire had been built up piecemeal, in different ways, over a long period.

The First British Empire

The first place to come under British control, not counting Ireland (1169), was Newfoundland, claimed by the explorer Humphrey Gilbert in 1585. Next, in the seventeenth century, British pirates captured islands in the West Indies; and in 1610 British traders claimed Virginia, which they wanted for its tobacco. In the eighteenth century, British traders made money out of supplying African slaves to these colonies, as a result of which they built trading forts along the coast of West Africa.

After 1610 also, the British East India Company opened 'factories' (trading posts) in India, which brought it into conflict with French traders. The defeat of the French brought Canada and land in India under British control, and the British found themselves with an 'Empire'.

This first phase of Empire came to an end with the American Revolution and the loss of the American Colonies (1783).

Motives for Empire

Historians disagree about why the British built up their huge Empire.

Some historians say the motive was money – the desire to get raw materials, and to sell to closed markets. Some historians have stressed the desire to bring Christianity to peoples regarded as 'savages'.

Certainly the motivation of individuals was varied. Many saw the Empire as a career opportunity. Others went to get land, or to avoid creditors, or for adventure – or just to shoot big game!

Britain used Australia as a place to send convicts. In the so-called Opium Wars (1839–42 and 1856–60), Britain obtained Hong Kong in China and forced the Chinese government to let British merchants trade drugs there.

Imperialism

In 1857, the Empire was shaken by the Indian Mutiny. An attempt to make Muslim soldiers use bullets greased with animal fat provoked a religious rebellion that covered most of northern India. The British government took rule in India away from the East India Company, and put the country under the control of the Indian Civil Service. In 1877 Queen Victoria was proclaimed 'Empress of India'.

This marked the start of 25 years of rapid empire-building. Four million square miles of land were added to the British Empire 1875–1900, most of it in Africa. This (the so-called 'scramble for Africa') involved wars with the Zulu tribes (1879) and the Dutch Boers (1881 and 1899–1902). It was during the second Boer War that the British invented concentration camps to imprison their enemies.

The leader of Britain's 'scramble for Africa' was Cecil Rhodes, who made a fortune from gold mining and conquered what came to be called Rhodesia (modern-day Zambia and Zimbabwe). Rhodes dreamed of a huge British Empire in Africa. This **Punch** *cartoon pictures him astride a map of Africa, with one foot on Cairo and the other on Cape Town.*

THINK ABOUT IT

1. Choose five important dates in the story of the British Empire.

2. Find four key motives that drove the British Empire-builders.

STOP AND REFLECT: Write an information text of 100 words, as if for an encyclopaedia, on 'The Growth of the British Empire' including all of the things you have identified. Finish by completing this sentence: 'The growth of the British Empire was characterised by…'.

What did the British think about the peoples of the Empire?

In 1895, Rudyard Kipling published *The Jungle Book*. Kipling had worked in India as a journalist, and his jungle was not the fun-filled place of the Disney film. In his story, the animals lived by 'the Law of the Jungle' – a brutal, never-ending war of killing and being killed. His story ended when the man-cub Mowgli learned how to control 'the Red Flower' (fire) and defeated the wicked tiger, Shere Khan.

The Jungle Book was **Darwinism** brought into a child's story – the survival of the fittest, and the natural superiority of humankind, but a superiority used for good against evil.

But what if Darwinism was brought into politics? Kipling believed completely that the white man was superior to those he called the 'lesser breeds'. But the white man, said Kipling, should not use his superiority for his own benefit. For Kipling, the true task of Empire was to 'impose peace, spare the underdog and pull down the proud'. He disliked missionaries, because they wanted to change the native people. He hated the Boers, because they treated the Africans cruelly.

SOURCE Ⓐ

The White Man's Burden

Take up the White Man's burden –
    Send forth the best ye breed –
Go, bind your sons to exile
    To serve your captives' need;
To wait, in heavy harness,
    On fluttered folk and wild –
Your new-caught sullen peoples,
    Half devil and half child.

Take up the White Man's burden –
    The savage wars of peace –
Fill full the mouth of Famine,
    And bid the sickness cease;
And when your goal is nearest
    (The end for others sought)
Watch sloth and heathen folly
    Bring all your hope to nought.

 Take up the White Man's burden,
    And reap his old reward –
The blame of those ye better
    The hate of those ye guard –
The cry of hosts ye humour
    (Ah, slowly!) toward the light:–
'Why brought ye us from bondage,
    Our loved Egyptian night?'

Take up the White Man's burden –
    Ye dare not stoop to less –
Nor call too loud on Freedom
    To cloak your weariness.
By all ye will or whisper,
    By all ye leave or do,
The silent sullen peoples
    Shall weigh your God and you.

Rudyard Kipling (1898).

THINK ABOUT IT

1. Study Kipling's poem in Source A, *The White Man's Burden.*

   - In what different ways does he describe the native peoples of the Empire?

   - What different tasks does he believe are the white man's job?

   - Read verse four carefully, then explain in your own words *why*, according to Kipling, the white man should behave like this.

2. Is the poem racist? Give at least two reasons for your answer.

SOURCE B

This American cartoon shows a stereotyped white colonialist carrying a stereotyped native African up a hill towards a School House.

Kipling's poem caused an immediate and furious reaction from people who thought it was racist and patronising.

Henry Labouchère, a Liberal politician, published a bitter and angry **parody** on Kipling's poem (Source D).

THINK ABOUT IT

1. Study Labouchère's poem in Source C, *The Brown Man's Burden*. Which do you think is his most bitter or angry statement? Explain what he means.

2. Study Source B carefully, explaining what you can see, then what the cartoon means. Is the cartoon racist?

3. Discuss as a class: If an Empire does good and right things, but for racist reasons, is it good or evil/right or wrong?

STOP AND REFLECT: Make notes (as five bullet points) on what the British thought about the peoples of Empire.

SOURCE C

The Brown Man's Burden

Pile on the brown man's burden
    To gratify your greed;
Go, clear away the 'niggers'
    Who progress would impede;
Be very stern, for truly
    'Tis useless to be mild
With new-caught, sullen peoples,
    Half devil and half child.

Pile on the brown man's burden;
    And, if ye rouse his hate,
Meet his old-fashioned reasons
    With theories up to date.
With shells and dumdum bullets
    A hundred times made plain
The brown man's loss must ever
    Imply the white man's gain.

Pile on the brown man's burden,
    compel him to be free;
Let all your manifestoes
    Reek with **philanthropy**.
And if with heathen folly
    He dares your will dispute,
Then, in the name of freedom,
    Don't hesitate to shoot.

Henry Labouchère, 25 February, 1899).

Should Britain pay compensation for the slave trade?

SOURCE A

This abolitionist cartoon of 1789 addresses the racist issue by asking people how they would feel if the slave owners were black and the slaves were white. A black slave owner beats a white slave, while behind them white slaves carry burdens and a black family feasts and dances. In the far distance, a fat British man says 'I have my rum, sugar and tobacco at the old price. I don't care if the slave trade is abolished.' On the right, a slave trader and an African king argue about the price of slaves.

The Triangular Trade

British colonists settling in America and the West Indies were hampered by a shortage of workers. And British traders saw a trading opportunity!

Loading up at Bristol or Liverpool with guns, gunpowder, brandy, cloth, glassware and iron goods – all things much in demand in Africa – they sailed to Africa to trade them for slaves.

Then they sailed with the slaves to the Americas (on the so-called 'Middle Passage'), and traded them there for rum, sugar and tobacco.

Rum, sugar and tobacco were much in demand back in Britain, so they then sailed back to Britain and sold them.

In theory, it was possible to make a profit on all three legs of the 'triangular trade', as it came to be called, although there was a real danger of shipwreck, and large numbers of slaves died of disease and despair while on the packed and filthy slave ships.

Abolition

The British traded slaves for 225 years, from 1562 to 1807, and Britain became the greatest slave-trading nation on earth. After 1750, British slave traders carried increasing numbers of slaves, and in the ten years after 1795, took three-quarters of a million slaves from Africa to the Americas. This enforced migration of the transatlantic slave trade was the largest **migration** in history.

After the 1770s, however, there grew up in England an anti-slavery movement, led by the MP William Wilberforce. Other prominent campaigners included black Africans who had been brought to England. Ottobah Cuguano and Olaudah Equiano are the most famous.

The campaigners conducted a brilliant campaign based on the principle of human rights (see Source A). 'Am I not a Man and a Brother?' asked their posters, almost 200 years before the Civil Rights marchers of twentieth-century America. In particular, they waged a brilliant **propaganda** war against the conditions on the Middle Passage, which has affected the way people think about the slave trade ever since.

In 1807, British traders were forbidden to carry slaves. The British abolished slavery in 1833. For the rest of the century, the British tried hard to stop the slave trade in Africa.

SOURCE Ⓑ

The Middle Passage – Olaudah Equiano Tells His Story

Quite overpowered with horror and anguish, I fell motionless on the deck and fainted. When I recovered a little, I asked if we were not to be eaten by those white men with horrible looks, red faces and long hair.

I was soon put down under the decks, and there I received such a greeting in my nostrils as I had never experienced in my life; so that, with the loathsomeness of the stench, and crying together, I became so sick and low that I was not able to eat, nor had I the least desire to taste anything. I now wished for the last friend, death, to relieve me.

Some of us had been permitted to stay on the deck for the fresh air. But now that the whole ship's cargo were confined together, it became absolutely pestilential. The closeness of the place, and the heat of the climate, added to the number in the ship, which was so crowded that each had scarcely room to turn himself, almost suffocated us.

I can now relate hardships which are inseparable from this accursed trade. The wretched situation was again aggravated by the chains, now unsupportable. The shrieks of the women, and the groans of the dying, rendered the whole a scene of horror almost inconceivable.

The Interesting Narrative of the Life of Olaudah Equiano the African (1789).

SOURCE Ⓒ

The Middle Passage

Nowhere in the annals of history has a people experienced such a long and traumatic ordeal as Africans during the Atlantic slave trade. Over the nearly four centuries of the trade, millions of African men, women, and children were savagely torn from their homeland, herded onto ships, and dispersed all over the so-called New World. Although there is no way to compute exactly how many people perished, it has been estimated that between 30 and 60 million Africans were subjected to this horrendous triangular trade system and that only one-third – if that – of those people survived...

Dr John Henrick Clarke
(http://www.juneteenth.com/middlep.htm).

THINK ABOUT IT

1. Using Source B make a list of all the horrors of the Middle Passage.

2. Although Source C was written by a modern historian, both Sources B and C are persuasive texts. Find all the powerful value-judgement words in the two sources that influence the reader to be horrified by the slave trade.

3. Take the role of one the following: an African king, a slave trader, an enslaved African, an African left behind, or an American planter who needs labourers.

   Working with a friend, prepare a statement about what 'you' think about the slave trade, and explain why.

In August–September 2001, the *United Nations World Conference Against Racism* was held at Durban in South Africa. One of the key speeches was an attack on the slave trade made by Zimbabwe's Minister of Justice.

There should emerge from this Conference a clear statement acknowledging the slave trade as a crime against humanity. The perpetrator countries must offer an apology for these crimes. A legal obligation to pay **reparations** should be placed on those countries who engaged in these evil practices.

P A Chinamasa

Britain opposed the use of the words 'crime against humanity' for the eighteenth-century slave trade (although prepared to apply it to slave traders today). In the end, the final conference declaration stated: 'Slavery and the slave trade were appalling tragedies...a crime against humanity', but it did *not* call on America and the countries of Europe to pay reparations.

If you had been at the Conference, what would you have said?

3. The slave trade ruined life even for those Africans who were *not* sold into slavery. In constant danger, many of them stopped bothering to work. Some sold their children into slavery for a bottle of brandy.

1. The slave trade ruined Africa. It took away half the population. It took the youngest, strongest people, and left the old, children and sick. Africa never recovered, was left open to conquest in the next century and *still* bears the economic and social scars.

2. The slave trade was not just done by white Europeans. The African kings captured slaves from other African tribes and sold them to the white traders. It was they, not the white traders, who controlled the trade. One American writer says that black Africans ought to apologise to black Americans for the slave trade.

4. What was so good about Africa before the slave trade? It was less economically developed, swept by tribal wars and had some vicious rulers. One American slave said she was *glad* to become a slave, because it meant she could not be eaten by a local cannibal tribe.

5. The slave trade put the African nations under the European nations. They suffered a crucial loss of power which led, in the end, to **colonialism**.

6. There is evidence that the slave trade did *not* ruin Africa – it was only a small factor in Africa's economy at the time.

7. Slavery was wrong *by nature*. There is no defence for it.

8. You cannot convict the slave traders of a 'crime against humanity' when no one at the time thought slavery was wrong, or understood the concept of a 'crime against humanity'

9. The slave trade treated the black slaves like animals, but it also brutalised the slave traders who became like animals in a different way.

10. The British were not the only nation that traded slaves – the French, Danish, Portuguese, Spanish and Arabs did it as well. After 1807, the British spent the rest of the century trying to *stop* the slave trade.

11. You cannot punish modern Europeans for something that happened hundreds of years ago, and that they would not have done themselves.

12. Stories of the cruelties and horror were hugely exaggerated by the abolitionists – it was not in the interests of the slave traders for slaves to die. No more people died on slave voyages than did on other voyages at that time, and traders took care of their slaves. There is evidence that some slave traders were popular with the slaves.

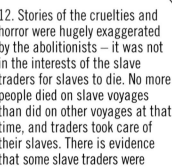

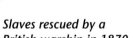
Slaves rescued by a British warship in 1870.

13. Slavery was racist. Only black Africans were captured and sold.

14. The slave trade gave the British huge wealth, and helped cause the Industrial Revolution, while Africa became impoverished.

THINK ABOUT IT

1. Study the statements. Which might be cited by the British delegation to the Racism Conference as arguments that the slave trade should not be called a 'crime against humanity'? Which might be cited by the African nations as arguments that Britain should pay compensation?

2. Hold your own 'Slave Trade Conference'. Ask your teacher to act as chairperson. Using the ideas on pages 78–81, and adding your own, debate if – and how – Britain should make amends for the slave trade.

STOP AND REFLECT: Using ICT, design a poster to hold up outside the Conference, to influence the delegates who are debating whether Britain ought to pay reparations for the slave trade.

This will be a persuasive text, so remember to include:
- A picture for emotional effect.
- A clever, powerful slogan-title that will grab people's attention.
- A short, clear sub-heading/phrase that 'unpacks' the slogan.
- Different types and sizes of font so that it can easily be read from a distance.

The Great Hunger – Research Study 1

'The Great Hunger' – in Gaelic An Gusta Mor.
In 'the years 1845–9 there was famine in Ireland'.

Ireland was England's oldest colony. By the Act of Union (1801), Britain took over direct rule of Ireland. However, in 1845 a potato blight from America destroyed the potato crop. The potato harvest failed again in 1846, 1847 and 1848. As a result, there was a famine.

The British response

Many British people did nothing, and some English Protestants welcomed the Hunger as God's punishment on Catholics. Other English people blamed Irish drunkenness and laziness for the famine. The economists of the time believed that free trade was the best way to create wealth, so they urged the government to do nothing.

However, the British government did take relief measures, more than it had ever done for any other famine in Ireland or England. It set up soup kitchens, and road-building schemes (which at one time employed 750,000 people). In all, the British Parliament provided assistance of £7 million. This amounted to only 3p per person per week, well short of what was needed. On the other hand, it represented some 3% of government expenditure, an amazing sum for the times (British government spending on foreign aid in 2000–1 was less than 1%). In addition, British charities also raised money, though some English missions demanded that the Irish convert to Protestantism before they would give them relief.

FACT FILE

Problems of Ireland before the Famine:

- Population: the Irish population was growing – from five million in 1780 to eight million in 1841.
- The system of inheritance: in England property was passed to the eldest son; in Ireland many farms were split between all the children. As a result, 45% of all farms in Ireland were five acres or less – too small to be efficient.
- 'Absentee' landlords: because the Irish had been conquered and their land confiscated, many landowners lived in England, and agents ran their estates. This led to corruption and neglect.
- The potato: two acres of potatoes could feed a family of eight for a year, and all that was needed to cultivate it was a spade. By 1845, many Irish poor lived on nothing but potatoes and milk.

SOURCE Ⓐ

That one million people should have died in what was then part of the richest and most powerful nation in the world is something that still causes pain as we reflect on it today. Those who governed in London at the time failed their people through standing by while a crop failure turned into a massive human tragedy.

Tony Blair (1997).

Aftermath

Perhaps a million people starved, and one-and-a-half million more emigrated to the USA. Disease followed famine. In 1851, the Irish population had fallen to six million.

Many Irish people accuse the English of **genocide** – of deliberately trying to exterminate the Irish. In 1997, Prime Minister Tony Blair apologised to the Irish people for the famine (Source A).

THINK ABOUT IT

1. What evidence can you find on page 83 that the Irish famine still affects people today'?

2. Why do you think Americans are particularly interested in the famine?

*In 1998 the Irish Community in the American city of Boston erected a memorial to the famine. Since 1996, New York schools have been required to teach the Great Hunger as 'a human rights abuse equal to the **Holocaust** and the slave trade'.*

SOURCE B

If the Irish find out that they can get free government grants, we shall have a system of beggars such as the world never knew... It forms no part of the functions of government to provide supplies of food...

God sent the calamity to teach the Irish a lesson.... The real evil with which we have to contend is not the physical evil of the famine, but the moral evil of the selfish, troublesome and violent character of the people...

Sir Charles Trevelyan, head of famine relief.

SOURCE C

God sent the Potato Blight but the English created the Famine. A million and a half of men, women and children, were carefully, prudently, and peacefully slain by the English government...

During all the famine years, Ireland was actually producing sufficient food to feed and clothe 18 millions of people; yet a ship sailing into an Irish port during the famine years with a cargo of grain was sure to meet six ships sailing out with a similar cargo...

John Mitchel, Last Conquest of Ireland (c.1873).

SOURCE D

Grain exports and imports: Ireland, 1844-8 ('000 tons)

	Exports	Imports	Net
1844	424	30	+394
1845	513	28	+485
1846	284	197	+87
1847	146	889	-743
1848	314	439	-125

Compare these figures to John Mitchel's claim in Source F that, during the famine, six grain ships left Ireland for every grain ship going to Ireland.

SOURCE E

The government did not prevent extra food from being imported. The government did not force exports to continue: Irish farmers chose to export their produce. Charitable societies were not prevented from feeding the poor.

The soc.culture.irish FAQ website

SOURCE F

*This **Punch** cartoon shows Ireland as a spoiled child demanding more and more help.*

SOURCE G

Nobody is suggesting that the government caused the famine. The suggestion is rather that, pushed by its contempt for Ireland, the government caused many people to die... Ireland was swept away by the most powerful and aggressive state the world had ever known. It suffered not from a potato fungus, but from conquest, theft, and slavery.

*Mark Thornton, **What Caused the Irish Potato Famine?***

SOURCE H

Although in Irish mythology much blame is heaped upon the British government for its failures to act in a generous manner, the private papers and records of genuinely good men tell a different story. There was no conspiracy to destroy the Irish people. In fact, several men compromised their political careers in order to alleviate the effects of the famine.

Jennifer Payne, **Ireland, Peel and Repeal.**

SOURCE J

In order to assess the role of the British government during the famine several key areas need to be addressed.

• First, what relief measures were introduced?

• Secondly, what were the motives behind the government's policy?

• Thirdly, and most importantly, how successful were the measures adopted in saving lives?

Paul Thompson, **The Irish Famine** *(1996).*

SOURCE I

In 1995 the Irish Parliament, the *Dáil Eireann,* debated the Great Hunger. This is what three of the members said:

• Mr M McDowell: Probably, most of our ancestors lived through that episode more or less unscathed and not as troubled by it as we would perhaps like to think… They were doing nothing very different from what ordinary people at the time were doing in England, quite unconscious of the cruelty that the underclass was suffering as a result of the famine.

• Mr Andrews: I find it very difficult to stomach, having studied the literature extensively over the summer, people suggesting that in some way we should show forgiveness [to the British] for what happened 150 years ago. From my reading, I was left with a feeling of deep anger and hurt. I know where the blame lies, which was, beginning and ending, with our then colonial masters.

• Mr Connor: I would not accuse the British Government of the time of maliciously and purposefully setting out to destroy the Irish race by way of the famine… There were local famines in Scotland, Cornwall and in the 1840s in places as close to London as Kent. What was the response of the Government? It was the same as its response to the famine in Ireland – it could not intervene. Those people acted not out of ill will or malice, but as a result of the thinking developed at that time.

THINK ABOUT IT

1. **Read Source J carefully, and then use the evidence on pages 82–85 to study the questions the writer suggests.**

2. **Read Source I. Paul Thompson writes: 'It would be a mistake to attempt to judge the actions taken 150 years ago without placing them in the context of the time.' Does this affect how you interpret events?**

3. **Debate as a class:**

   (a) Were the British to blame for the Great Hunger?

   (b) Even if the British were not to blame for the Irish famine, can Britons be proud of the way the government handled the famine?

   (c) Were the British guilty of genocide in Ireland?

STOP AND REFLECT: Write a brief discursive text (including argument and counter-argument) as if for an editorial in a newspaper, on the topic: 'Should the British Prime Minister have apologised for the Irish famine?'

The British Rule in India – Research Study 2

SOURCE A

Every summer, the entire government administration moved more than a thousand miles from Calcutta to the hill town of Simla, where the climate was cooler. This picture shows the post office at Simla, with the mail tonga – a two-wheeled covered wagon – outside. The drivers prided themselves on being the best postal service in the world, and got the mail through storm and rain, torrents and hillslides, hail, and snow, even at the risk of their lives.

SOURCE B

The Indian Civil Service

For integrity and efficiency, the Indian **Civil Service** was almost certainly the finest civil service man has yet devised. Its incorruptibility became a byword among Indians. A story from the early twentieth century shows this. A young officer ran out of money and borrowed £50 from a yak owner, in exchange for an IOU on a sheet of newspaper. Almost a year later the IOU was presented with the marks of many transactions on it, having passed through several hands all over Central Asia as a piece of currency that would be honoured on demand.

G Moorhouse, India Britannica (1983).

Queen Victoria declared herself 'Empress' of India, so it is arguable that here was probably Britain's 'best effort' at **imperialism**. The sources that follow will allow you to form a view of how well the British ruled India. As you study pages 86–90, therefore, note all the good things you can find about British rule in India, and also all the bad things you come across.

Was the British government of India of a high quality?

SOURCE C

British India

The Raj was a bluff. Some 300 million Indians were ruled by barely 1500 administrators of the Indian Civil Service. If the Indian people had chosen to throw off their overlords, there would have been little to prevent them.

Zachary Nunn, The British Raj.

SOURCE D

Good Works

British brains, British enterprise and British money had transformed India. Innumerable bridges, more than 40,000 miles of railway, 70,000 miles of surfaced roads, testify to the skill and industry of British engineers. Irrigation works on a stupendous scale have brought 30,000 acres under cultivation. Thanks to improved sanitation, to a higher standard of living, to irrigation, to canal building, to the development of transport, and to thoughtfully thought-out schemes for relief work, famines have now virtually disappeared.

Sir John Marriot (1932).

SOURCE E

Government Spending, 1913-14

Administration (ICS)	27%
Armed forces	25%
Education	4%
Medical/public health	2%
Railways/irrigation/roads	17%
Other	25%

SOURCE F

British Interests

The British were interested in the kind of growth that would help them back in Britain. They needed the railways to transport the raw materials to the ports.

Dr Ashak Mitra, an Indian writer.

SOURCE G

Many of the crops grown by Indian farmers were grown to supply raw materials for the factories of Great Britain. This picture shows the sorting of Indigo c.1900.

SOURCE H

Care and Famine

We do not care for the people of India. Do we even care enough to know about their daily lives and lingering death from causes which we could so well remove? We have taken their lands and their rulers into our charge for State reasons of our own…But for their daily lives and deaths we do not as a nation care.

Florence Nightingale (1878).

◆ *1877 was a year of famine, the fourth in ten years. About a million people died of starvation, but another five million died from the cholera that swept through the relief camps. A fund was opened in London, and the British government sent grain ships.*

THINK ABOUT IT

Read Sources A–H:

1. List all the instances of good government you can find.

2. Find evidence which proves that the British were only serving their own interests.

3. What is the significance of Source C?

4. Discuss with a friend: Were the British good rulers of India?

Was Lord Curzon a good Viceroy of India, 1899–1905?

SOURCE I

This photograph shows Lord Curzon with an Indian prince, the Maharajah of Gwalior.
• *Curzon was educated at Eton and Oxford. He worked a 12–14-hour day. He extended the irrigation schemes, initiated a programme of school building, and restored many historical buildings (including the Taj Mahal). He believed that 'There has never been anything so great in the world's history as the British Empire, so great an instrument for the good of humanity'.*
• *What does this photograph suggest about his attitude to the Indian princes?*

SOURCE J

Responsibility

To fight for the right, to hate the imperfect, to care nothing for flattery, reputation or abuse. Never to let your enthusiasm be soured or your courage grow dim.

> *Lord Curzon, speech when leaving India on how he had tried to do his job as Viceroy (1905).*

SOURCE K

Curzon and The Army

Some drunks from a crack cavalry unit, the 9th Lancers, beat an Indian to death, and the officers of the regiment tried to whitewash the affair. These were sons of the peerage with powerful influence at home, and they let it be known that they were prepared to use all their connections to stop his interference. Regardless of what back-stabbing might follow from London, Curzon had every Lancer recalled from leave whether the man was in India or not, every officer's leave stopped for the next six months, and the regiment reprimanded in the strongest terms — a disgrace that was soon the talk of the whole army.

'The argument seems to be that a native's life does not count… I have set my face like flint against such evil,' Curzon wrote.

Within a few years of Curzon's stand, such assaults were unheard of.

> *G Moorhouse, India Britannica (1983).*

SOURCE L

Curzon's Durbar, 1903
The Durbar (an Indian word meaning 'court-reception')
was designed to celebrate the accession of King Edward
VII. The Durbar area was so large that it needed a
railway, five miles long, to take people round the site.
A huge marquee housed a massive exhibition of Indian
culture. The programme lasted ten days and included
games, displays, military bands, troop reviews, medal
ceremonies and an open-air religious service (Christian).
At night there were balls and banquets.

The highlight was the grand state entry on New Year's
Day, when thousands of princes, retainers, soldiers,
officials (and elephants) paraded past Lord and Lady
Curzon to proclaim the new king Edward VII. The
parade was watched by more than a million people
and finished with a salute of 101 guns.

THINK ABOUT IT

Using Sources I–L:

- List everything Curzon did of which Britons should be proud.

- Suggest examples where his rule of India was unsatisfactory or insensitive.

Was Curzon a good ruler of India?

Were the British in India racist?

SOURCE Ⓜ

Arrogance

An advanced native, of independent character, once complained to me that most Englishmen appeared to him to walk about the world with an air as if God Almighty intended the whole universe to be English.

Monier Williams (c.1875)

◆ *Williams was a Professor at Oxford University.*

SOURCE Ⓝ

Exclusion in the India Civil Service

There was nothing on paper to stop an Indian from competing in the Civil Service examinations, but to do so he had to sit the exams in London and go to a British University. His family had to pay £1000. In a personnel of 1200 not more than 50 were natives.

S Reed, The India I Knew (1952).

SOURCE Ⓞ

In India, but not of it

We were looked after by Indian servants and we met a great many Indians, but once you stepped inside the home you were back in Britain. We brought with us in our home lives almost exact replicas of the sort of life that upper-middle-class people lived in England at that time.

I can't really say that we took an awful lot from India.

The wife of an English official in the Indian Civil Service.

SOURCE Ⓟ

A British family with their Indian servants.

SOURCE Ⓠ

Class not Race

The British Empire was not based on race, but depended as much on the colour-blind ranking of social class. An aristocratic official would feel much more in common with an Indian who went to the same public school as he did, than with an Englishman who was his social inferior.

David Cannadine, Orientalism (2001).

THINK ABOUT IT

Study Sources M–Q. Were the British in India racist?

STOP AND REFLECT: Write a brief discursive text (including argument and counter-argument) on the topic: 'Was British rule in India good?'

Pulling it Together

Should Britons be proud of the British Empire?

From an Internet Forum

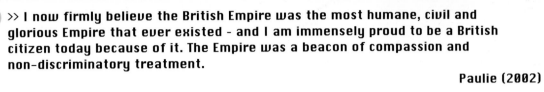

>> I now firmly believe the British Empire was the most humane, civil and glorious Empire that ever existed - and I am immensely proud to be a British citizen today because of it. The Empire was a beacon of compassion and non-discriminatory treatment.

Paulie (2002)

>> Why is it immoral for Nazi 2 occupy Europe only, but not immoral 4 Brits to occupy the world? Shame!

Questioner (2002)

Every time the National Curriculum is revised, there is a debate in the newspapers about whether pupils ought to study the British Empire. Traditionalists argue that the Empire is a glorious part of British history which ought to be celebrated; radicals argue that it is an insult to the ethnic groups in our communities. Your task is to decide what you think about the British Empire, and to enter into that debate.

Stage 1 Preparation

1. Scan back over pages 73–91 with a friend. Make two lists: one of all the things that you think make the British Empire something to be proud of, the other of all those things that you think were shameful.

2. Have a class discussion: 'Should Britons be proud of the British Empire?'

3. Talking with a small group of friends, discuss whether you think the British Empire ought to be included in the National Curriculum as something to study.

Stage 2 Writing the letter

4. Imagine you are your parent! Write a letter to your headteacher saying why you think your child ought/ought not to have to study the British Empire in History.

(a) The basic letter *will express an opinion, and give some facts about the British Empire.*

(b) A better letter *will give an opinion about whether pupils ought to study the British Empire, supporting the argument with a reason, and giving some facts about the British Empire.*

(c) A very good letter *will give an opinion about whether pupils ought to study the British Empire, supporting the argument with a number of reasons, and using facts about the British Empire to support the argument.*

(d) The best letter *will realise that it is profitable to study both good and bad things in history.*

POSTSCRIPT
What did Jack the Ripper ever do for us?

More than the legend will survive.

JOHNNY
DEPP
HEATHER
GRAHAM

FROM
HELL

OCTOBER

From Hell had an '18' certificate.

'One day men will look back and say that I gave birth to the twentieth century.'

Jack the Ripper, in the film From Hell, 2001.

In 2001, the film *From Hell*, starring Johnny Depp and Heather Graham, gave the modern film version of the story of Jack the Ripper.

The film brings the Ripper story to the modern viewer. But it does not tell the same story as was told to the people of London in 1888.

In the modern film:

- Mary Kelly and the other prostitutes are friends. They are being murdered because they know about the secret marriage of Prince Albert Victor to a commoner. It is a 'Rippergate' scandal that goes to the very top – Queen Victoria knows about it and condones it.

- The murders are committed by Dr William Gull (the Royal Family's doctor) who is dangerously mad and believes himself to be equal to God. At the end of the film, he is silenced by being given a **lobotomy** (although lobotomies were not performed until ten years later).

- The bodies are mutilated – there are explicit scenes of frenzied bloodlust – with damage to the private parts.

- Whitechapel is shown as being a very poor area.

- Inspector Abberline is a drug addict with psychic abilities – a maverick, disliked by the establishment. Although he finds out the truth, he is prevented by a 'cover-up' from making it public.

- Abberline falls in love with Mary Kelly. Helped by him, she escapes and lives happily by the seaside with her child.

When we studied the Ripper murders on pages 4–6, we suggested that the story could never have come from an earlier age. The way *From Hell* treats its subject tells us that neither could it have come from our modern age.

FACT FILE

The Washington Sniper – a modern serial killer

In October 2002, the people of Washington were terrorised by a serial killer.

- The killer shot ten people and wounded three others, using a high-velocity rifle with telescopic sights.
- The drive-by murders were apparently random and pointless – e.g. a woman loading shopping into the boot of her car; a child arriving at his school.
- As the killer was using a car, the shootings occurred over a wide area of Maryland and Virginia.
- The case created immense media interest. TV news ratings soared.
- Police were baffled. They followed 1650 credible leads and watched hours of CCTV tapes. They offered a reward of $240,000.

- John Muhammad (42), the killer, and John Malvo, his 17-year-old accomplice, were captured after a tip-off connected the killings to an earlier robbery in Alabama, at which Malvo left a fingerprint. After a nationwide radio and TV appeal to the public, a passing motorist noticed the killers' car, and the police arrested the two men without a struggle.
- Muhammad was a Gulf War veteran who was an expert marksman in the army. He had converted to Islam in 1985 and was said to approve of the 11 September World Trade Centre terrorist attack. He had a history of mental instability.
- Some people, however, blamed an 'undercurrent of rage' in American society, caused by social inequality, poverty and unemployment.

THINK ABOUT IT

1. Compare the nineteenth-century story of Jack the Ripper (on pages 4–6) with the modern story of the 'Washington sniper'.

    (a) What aspects of the two stories are similar?

    (b) What is different?

    (c) Why did the US police catch the Washington sniper, where the nineteenth-century British police failed to catch the Ripper?

2. Discuss how the difference between the stories provides historians with information about what has – and what has not – changed between 1888 and 2002. Think particularly about:

    - science and technology

    - attitudes

    - living conditions

    - religion

    - public opinion

    - attitudes to the Army, and to foreigners.

STOP AND REFLECT:

Did the Ripper – as the film *From Hell* claims – 'give birth to the twentieth century'?

GLOSSARY

abatement Reduction.

agent provocateur A French phrase meaning: 'someone who provokes'. Government spies who organised plots, then arrested those they had persuaded to take part.

agnostic A person who does not deny the existence of God, but says we can never know whether a God exists.

almshouses In the nineteenth century, houses provided free of rent for old people.

anaesthetics Painkillers.

antibiotics Drugs that seek out and kill specific germs.

antiseptic A chemical that kills germs.

aristocracy/aristocratic The lords/noble classes.

atheist Believes God does not exist.

ballot A vote in an election made in secret and put into a 'ballot box'.

biased Tending to support only one side of the argument – misrepresenting the facts to support that side.

Budget The statement, by the **Chancellor of the Exchequer**, of the government's spending for the next year.

census A count of the population, taken every ten years.

Chancellor of the Exchequer The government minister who looks after the government's finance and taxation.

Chartists People who tried to get the government to accept a 'Charter' (petition) which would give ordinary people political rights.

cholera A deadly disease of the bowels, caught from germs in drinking water.

Civil Service The government officials who run the administration of the government – as opposed to the MPs, who make the laws that the Civil Service have to administer.

civilised/civilisation The way a people/society lives, especially all its finer beliefs and achievements.

colonialism Building up an empire by taking over/conquering other countries.

Communism/Communists The belief that no person has the right to own land or a factory, and that factories make 'wage-slaves' of the workers.

constituency An area/place that elects a single MP to Parliament.

constitution The system of government in a country.

Darwinism Belief in the theory of **evolution**.

democracy Government by the people – usually by voting for their government.

dispensaries Chemists, giving out medicines.

dole Unemployment pay.

emissions Smoke and fumes.

evolution The belief that humankind developed slowly from single-cell creatures over millions of years – the opposite of 'creation' which believes that God made the world.

genocide The attempt to kill a whole race of people.

habeas corpus A Latin phrase meaning: 'you may have body'; the law which prevents imprisonment without being charged with a specific crime.

Holocaust The Nazi attempt to kill all the Jews in the Second World War.

imperialism The desire to gain an Empire.

independence When countries gain their freedom from control by another nation or Empire.

Industrial Revolution 'Industry' is the way people make things. A revolution is a complete change-around from the past – in industry, society or politics – often violent. So the Industrial Revolution was a complete change in the way things were made.

innovation Using inventions to increase or improve production.

inoculation Giving a dead or weakened form of a germ to a person, so that the person is able to build up immunity to that illness.

investment Putting money into industry to buy new machines or buildings.

'less eligibility' The principle that – in order to stop it being attractive to lazy people – poor relief had to be less attractive than the worst job and the poorest existence.

lobotomy Operation to detach the front lobes of the brain from the rest of the brain – it left patients dull and lethargic.

midden A muck-heap.

migration Movement of numbers of people from one place to another.

missionaries People of a certain religion who go to another country to try to make converts.

oath When you swear something (e.g. on the Bible).

parody Copying the style of a text, often with the intent to mock it or challenge it.

parson Vicar/priest of a parish.

philanthropy Charity/kindness – literally 'love of one's fellow man'.

picket When trade unionists stand outside a factory during a strike, and try to persuade other workers there to go on strike too.

privy Nineteenth-century word for a toilet, usually outside.

propaganda Putting out information to persuade and influence people to support your case.

property qualification Before 1858, MPs had to own a certain amount of land.

prostitute A woman who gives sex for money.

Public Health Measures taken by the government to give people a clean water supply, sewerage, healthy food, etc.

racist/racism The hatred/criticism of another group of people solely because of their race, racial traditions and the colour of their skin.

reparations Punitive payments to repair damage done.

revival A sudden growth in enthusiasm for religion.

Royal Commission A government enquiry.

Salvation Army 'Salvation' is the religious experience when Christians believe that Jesus Christ has saved them from going to Hell. The Salvation Army believed they were fighting against evil in a battle for the souls of men.

sanitation Providing sewers.

slum An area of very poor housing.

squalor Dirty, disgusting and poor conditions.

Suffrage (Suffragists and Suffragettes) 'Suffrage' is possessing the vote. The Suffragists campaigned for this peacefully; the Suffragettes used violence to try to get the vote for women.

syphilis A sexually-transmitted disease. In extreme cases, it sends the sufferer mad.

technology/technological Production methods.

tract A religious pamphlet, printed to give to potential converts.

Trade Unions Unions of workers, set up to get better conditions and wages for their members.

transportation (In the penal sense) being sent to Australia as punishment for a crime.

typhoid A deadly disease caused by germs in drinking water.

utilitarianism The philosophy that argued that government ought to follow the course which provided the greatest happiness for the greatest number of people, at the expense of minority rights.

INDEX